A-Z TOP

CONTENT

Map Pages	2-33
Key to Map Pages	Back Cover
Index selected Places of Interest	

REFERENCE

A Road	A380
B Road	B3199
Dual Carriageway	
One-way Street Traffic flow on A roads is indicated by a heavy line on the drivers' left.	
Restricted Access	
Pedestrianized Road	
Track & Footpath	
Residential Walkway	
Railway	Station, Heritage Sta., Level Crossing, Tunnel
Beaches	
Built-up Area	NEW ST.
Local Authority Boundary	
National Park Boundary	
Postcode Boundary	
Map Continuation	16

Car Park Selected	P
Church or Chapel	†
Fire Station	
Hospital	H
House Numbers A & B Roads only	218 17
Information Centre	i
National Grid Reference	290
Police Station	▲
Post Office	★
Toilet with facilities for the disabled	
Educational Establishment	
Hospital or Hospice	
Industrial Building	
Leisure or Recreational Facility	
Place of Interest	
Public Building	
Shopping Centre or Market	
Other Selected Buildings	

Scale 1:15,840

0 — ¼ — ½ Mile

0 — 250 — 500 — 750 Metres — 1 Kilometre

4 inches (10.16 cm) to 1 mile
6.31 cm to 1 km

Geographers' A-Z Map Company Ltd.

Head Office:
Fairfield Road, Borough Green, Sevenoaks, Kent, TN15 8PP
Telephone 01732 781000 (General Enquiries & Trade Sales)

Showrooms:
44 Gray's Inn Road, London, WC1X 8HX
Telephone 020 7440 9500 (Retail Sales)
www.a-zmaps.co.uk

This map is based upon Ordnance Survey mapping with the permission of The Controller of Her Majesty's Stationery Office.

Edition 3 2000

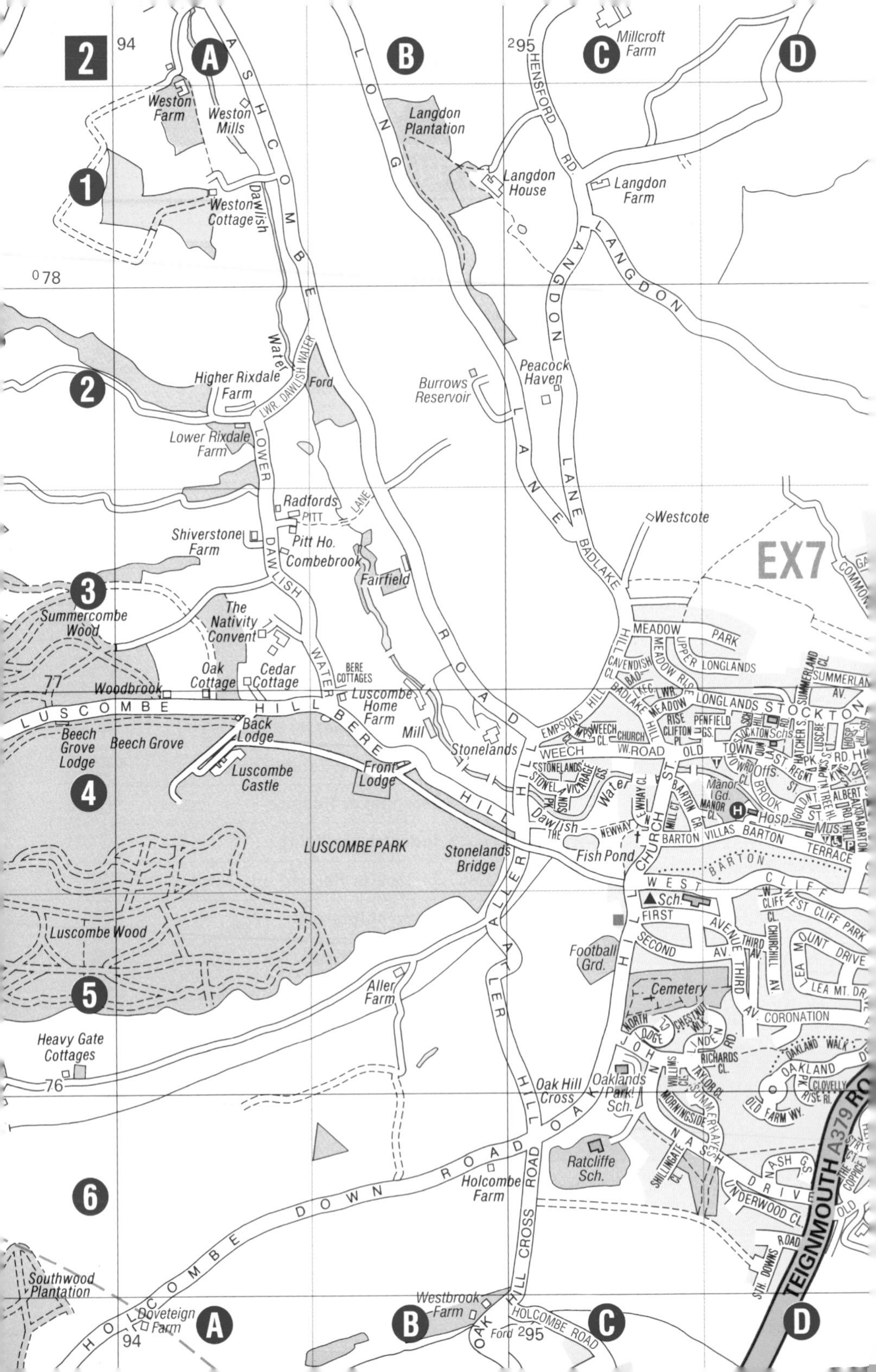

2
A
B
C
D
94
295
Weston Farm
Weston Mills
Weston Cottage
Langdon Plantation
Langdon House
Langdon Farm
Millcroft Farm
Higher Rixdale Farm
Lower Rixdale Farm
Ford
Burrows Reservoir
Peacock Haven
Radfords
Shiverstone Farm
Pitt Ho.
Combebrook
Fairfield
Westcote
EX7
Summercombe Wood
The Nativity Convent
Oak Cottage
Cedar Cottage
Bere Cottages
Woodbrook
Luscombe Home Farm
Mill
Stonelands
Beech Grove Lodge
Beech Grove
Back Lodge
Luscombe Castle
Front Lodge
LUSCOMBE PARK
Stonelands Bridge
Fish Pond
Luscombe Wood
Football Grd.
Cemetery
Aller Farm
Heavy Gate Cottages
Oak Hill Cross
Oaklands Park Sch.
Ratcliffe Sch.
Holcombe Farm
Southwood Plantation
Doveteign Farm
Westbrook Farm
Ford
LUSCOMBE HILL
BERE HILL
ASHCOMBE
LONG ROAD
LANGDON LANE
HENSFORD RD.
LANGDON
BADLAKE
HOLCOMBE DOWN ROAD
OAK HILL CROSS ROAD
HOLCOMBE ROAD
ALLER HILL
TEIGNMOUTH A379 RD
CHURCH HILL
WEST CLIFF
BARTON VILLAS
BARTON TERRACE
CORONATION AV.
OAKLAND WALK
UNDERWOOD CL.
NASH DRIVE

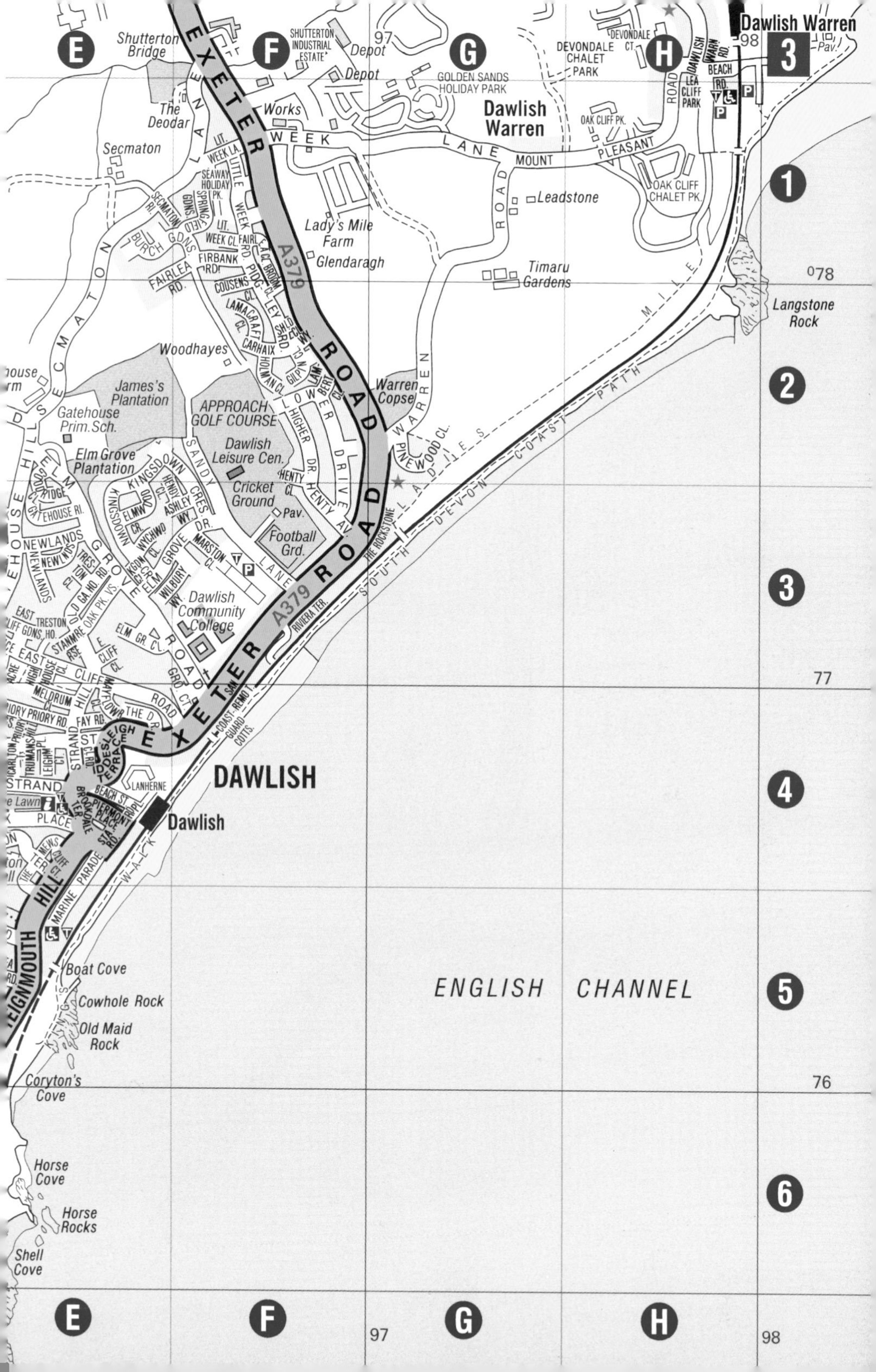

Dawlish Warren
3
E
F
G
H
Shutterton Bridge
SHUTTERTON INDUSTRIAL ESTATE
Depot
Depot
GOLDEN SANDS HOLIDAY PARK
DEVONDALE CHALET PARK
Dawlish Warren
Works
The Deodar
Secmaton
EXETER ROAD
WEEK LANE
MOUNT PLEASANT
Leadstone
OAK CLIFF CHALET PK.
Lady's Mile Farm
Glendaragh
Timaru Gardens
Langstone Rock
Woodhayes
James's Plantation
Gatehouse Prim.Sch.
APPROACH GOLF COURSE
Dawlish Leisure Cen.
Cricket Ground
Elm Grove Plantation
Warren Copse
Football Grd.
Dawlish Community College
A379
SOUTH DEVON COAST PATH
LADIES MILE
DAWLISH
Dawlish
TEIGNMOUTH HILL
MARINE PARADE
Boat Cove
Cowhole Rock
Old Maid Rock
Coryton's Cove
Horse Cove
Horse Rocks
Shell Cove
ENGLISH CHANNEL
1
2
3
4
5
6
97
98
078
77
76

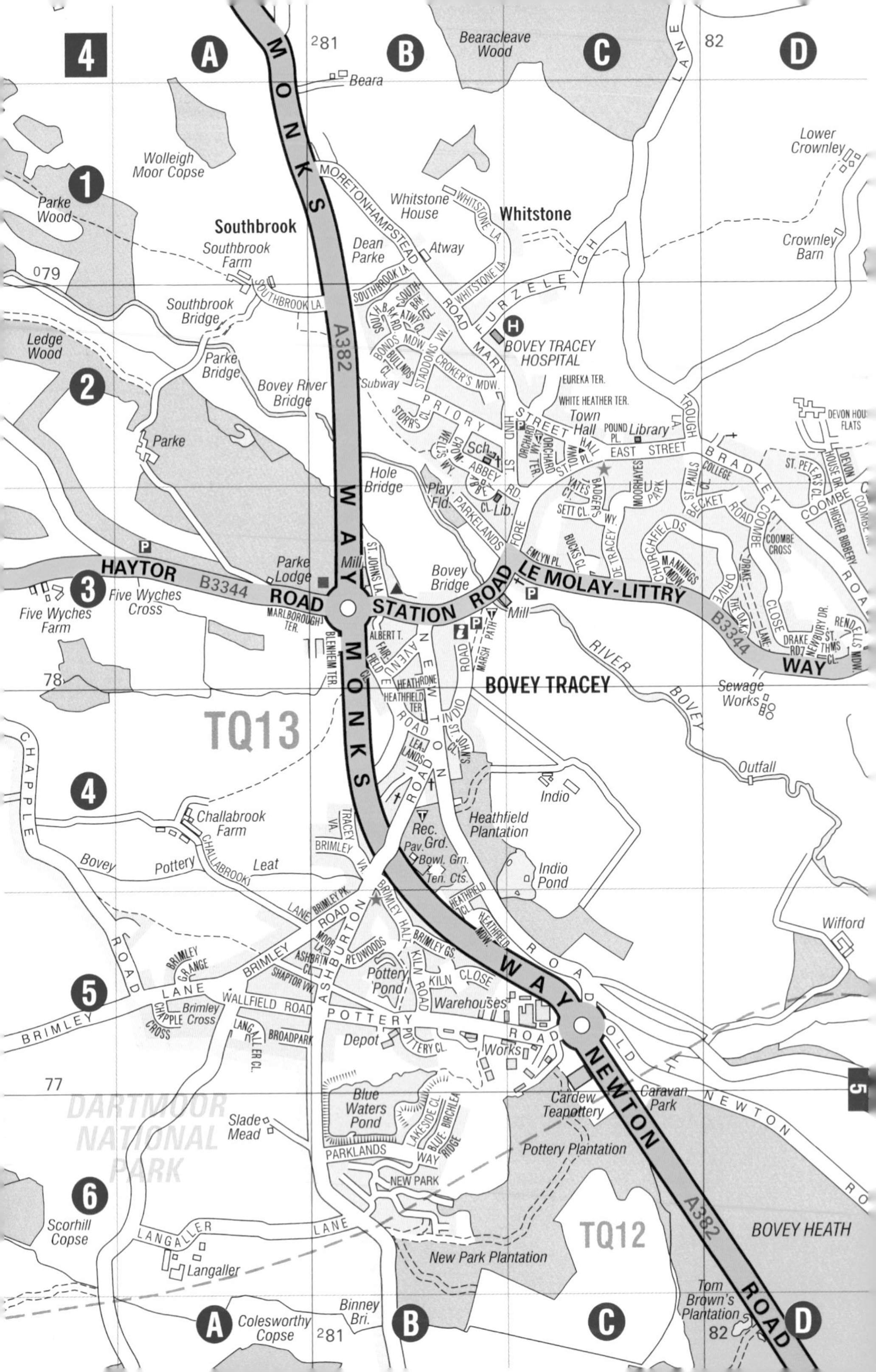
A
B
C
D
281
82
Bearacleave Wood
Beara
Lower Crownley
Wolleigh Moor Copse
Parke Wood
Southbrook
Southbrook Farm
Whitstone House
Whitstone
Dean Parke
Atway
Crownley Barn
079
MONKS WAY
MORETONHAMPSTEAD ROAD
WHITSTONE LA.
FURZELEIGH LANE
SOUTHBROOK LA.
Southbrook Bridge
Ledge Wood
Parke Bridge
Bovey River Bridge
A382
Subway
BOVEY TRACEY HOSPITAL
EUREKA TER.
WHITE HEATHER TER.
Town Hall
Library
EAST STREET
TROUGH LA.
BRADLEY ROAD
DEVON HOUSE FLATS
Parke
PRIORY
Hole Bridge
Play. Fld.
Sch.
Lib.
FORE ST.
HIND ST.
PARKELANDS
BADGERS WY.
MOORHAYES
PARK
CHURCHFIELDS
COOMBE CROSS
COOMBE WAY
HAYTOR ROAD
B3344
Parke Lodge
Mill
Bovey Bridge
STATION ROAD
LE MOLAY-LITTRY WAY
Five Wyches Cross
Five Wyches Farm
MARLBOROUGH TER.
BLENHEIM TER.
Mill
MARSH PATH
RIVER BOVEY
78
BOVEY TRACEY
Sewage Works
TQ13
CHAPPLE ROAD
NEWTON ROAD
HEATHFIELD TER.
INDIO
Outfall
Indio
Heathfield Plantation
Challabrook Farm
Rec. Grd.
Pav.
Bowl. Grn.
Ten. Cts.
Indio Pond
Bovey Pottery Leat
CHALLABROOK LANE
BRIMLEY VA.
ASHBURTON ROAD
Wifford
BRIMLEY LANE
Pottery Pond
KILN CLOSE
Warehouses
POTTERY ROAD
WALLFIELD ROAD
Brimley Cross
CHAPPLE CROSS
BROADPARK
Depot
Works
OLD NEWTON ROAD
77
DARTMOOR NATIONAL PARK
Slade Mead
Blue Waters Pond
Cardew Teapottery
Caravan Park
Pottery Plantation
PARKLANDS WAY
NEW PARK
Scorhill Copse
LANGALLER LANE
Langaller
TQ12
BOVEY HEATH
New Park Plantation
Tom Brown's Plantation
Colesworthy Copse
Binney Bri.
1
2
3
4
5
6
5

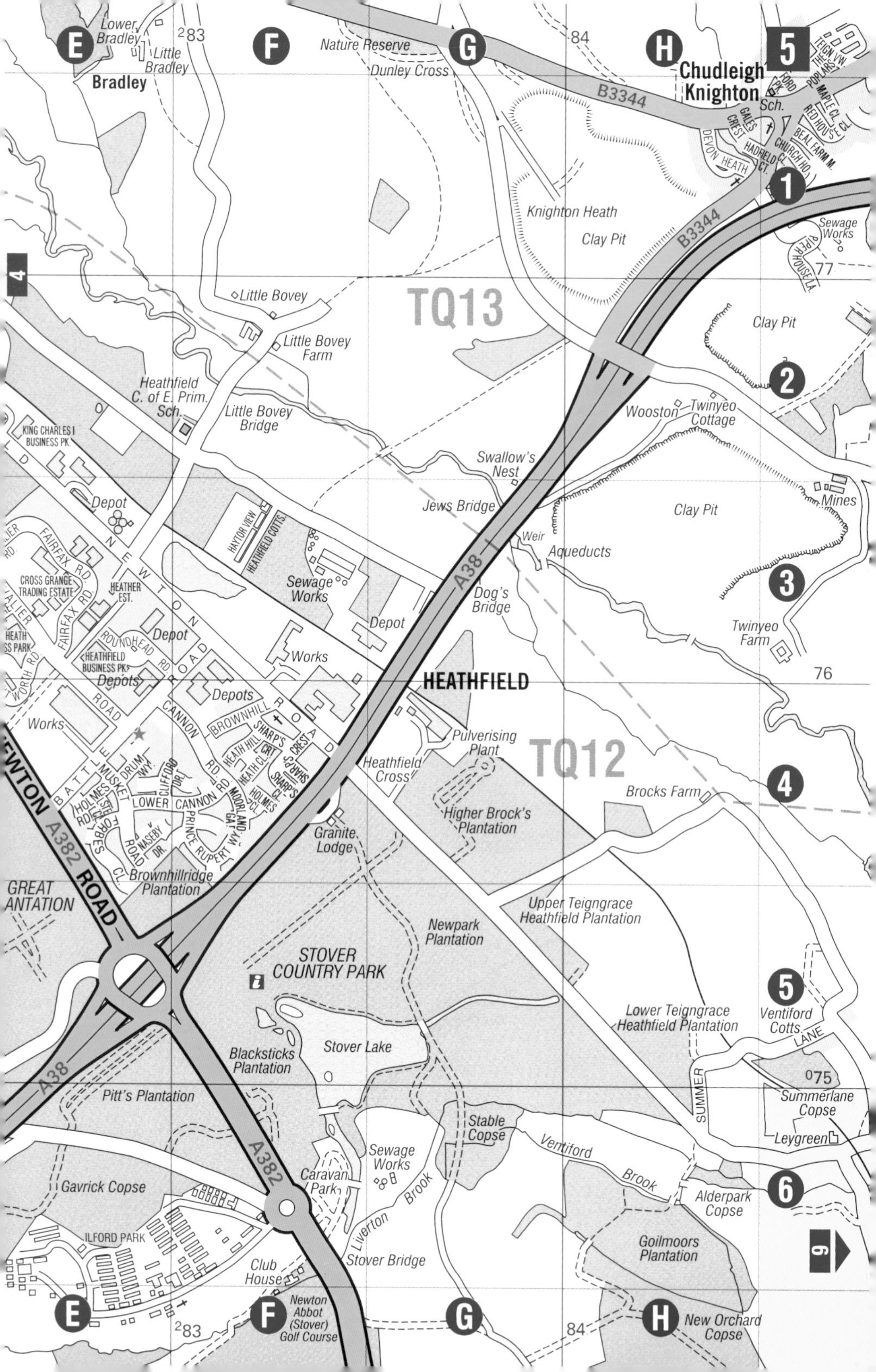

E
F
G
H
5
Lower Bradley
Little Bradley
Bradley
283
Nature Reserve
Dunley Cross
84
Chudleigh Knighton
B3344
Knighton Heath
Clay Pit
B3344
Sewage Works
77
4
TQ13
Clay Pit
Little Bovey
Little Bovey Farm
Heathfield C. of E. Prim. Sch.
Little Bovey Bridge
Wooston
Twinyeo Cottage
Swallow's Nest
Jews Bridge
Clay Pit
Mines
Weir
Aqueducts
KING CHARLES I BUSINESS PK.
Depot
HAYTOR VIEW
HEATHFIELD COTTS.
Sewage Works
Depot
A38
Dog's Bridge
CROSS GRANGE TRADING ESTATE
HEATHER EST.
Depot
NEWTON ROAD
Works
Twinyeo Farm
HEATHFIELD BUSINESS PK.
Depots
Depots
HEATHFIELD
76
Works
BROWNHILL
CANNON
Pulverising Plant
TQ12
Heathfield Cross
Brocks Farm
Higher Brock's Plantation
Granite Lodge
Brownhillridge Plantation
GREAT ANTATION
NEWTON A382 ROAD
Upper Teigngrace Heathfield Plantation
Newpark Plantation
STOVER COUNTRY PARK
Lower Teigngrace Heathfield Plantation
Ventiford Cotts.
LANE
SUMMER
Blacksticks Plantation
Stover Lake
075
Summerlane Copse
A38
Pitt's Plantation
Stable Copse
Leygreen
Ventiford
Brook
A382
Sewage Works
Caravan Park
Gavrick Copse
Brook
Alderpark Copse
ILFORD PARK
Liverton
Goilmoors Plantation
9
Stover Bridge
Club House
Newton Abbot (Stover) Golf Course
283
84
New Orchard Copse
1
2
3
4
5
6

6
A
B
C
D
075
285
86
Summerlane Copse
LANE
SUMMER LA.
SUMMER
Leygreen
Ventford Bri.
TEMPLAR WAY
Clay Works
PRESTON
Manor Farm
Higher Preston Cross
Manor Cottage
Burnells
Mortimer's Farm
Sampson's Farm
JOHN ACRES LANE
Clay Pit
1
Alderpark Copse
5
Goilmoors Plantation
New Orchard Copse
Ventiford Brook
2
Abbrook Pond
Depot
Lower Preston Cross
Abrook Bridge
Stream
B3193
Cycle Track
Ugbrooke
Rectory
Locks Bridge
Hearders
74
Clay Works
Teigngrace
SCHOOL RD.
SCHOOL COTTS.
Lower Lodge
3
Broadway Clay Works
ROAD
Clay Pit
Twelve Oaks Farm
Butland's Plantation
Breakwater
Teign Bridge
Depot
BROADWAY
Forches Cross
LANE
GREYCOAT
Woodside
Teignbridge Crossing
Clay Pit
RIVER
BOVEY
4
Playing Field
St. Mary's
Orchid Paradise
Burnham Nurseries
The Little House
Playing Field
Clay Cellars
TQ12
Teignbridge Gate
Clay Pit
73
Blatchford
Segar's Plantation
Brook
Blatchford Brook
TRACEY
A382
ROAD
EXETER
Berry Knowles
Sandford Orleigh Farm
5
Clay Pit
RINGSLADE
Linden Lea
TEIGN
Club House
Ringslade
Quarry (dis.)
ROAD
Whitehill House
EXETER
West Golds Mine
ORLEIGH
WHITEHILL CL.
East Gold Mar Clay Work
Daracombe (Halls of Res.)
6
Highweek
Lower Loady Park
WHITEHILL
Res. (cov.)
BELVEDERE RD.
HOWTON RD.
GAZE HILL
Gaze Hill
RINGSLADE CL.
WHITEHILL COTTS.
War Memorial
ROAD
AVENUE
ORLEIGH PK.
Kingsteig Bridg
Nature Reserve
MILE END
RD. HIGHWEEK
VILLAGE
HIGHWEEK CL.
CHURCH
PATH
Sandford Orleigh
Quay
MARSH
A383
Depot
Kingsteignton Road Bridge
72
NORMAN CL.
JETTY
HAMILTON DR.
VIEW
BLENHEIM CL.
Castle Dyke
A
PITT HILL ROAD
11
SANDFORD
C
ROAD
D
285
Prim. Sch.
B
Coombeshead College
Play.
86
SEYMOUR
ROAD
HILL PARK RD.

7
E
F
G
H
87
88
075
74
73
72
1
2
3
4
5
6
12
SANDYGATE
Sandygate Bridge
Lower Sandygate
HIGHER SANDYGATE
SANDYGATE
EAGLE CLOSE
MILL
ORCHRD CL.
Stream
Ponswine
Little Lyndridge Farm
Great Hill
Rhapsody
Lenada
Lyndale
HESTOW
LANE
LINDRIDGE
Lindridge Hill Cottages
Torhill Cottage
Lodge
HILL
ROAD
King's Wood
Vaseford Copse
Durley Wood
Buckley Wood
Whitelands
Reservoir (covered)
Quarry (dis.)
Coombes End
Bickleyball
Colladown
Coombesend Wood
Coombes End
Woodlands
COOMBESEND RD.
COOMBESEND ROAD EAST
A381
TEIGNMOUTH RD.
TEIGNMOUTH
Ware Barton
WARE BARTON CARAVAN SITE
B-U-R-D-O-U-N-S
W-A-Y
WAY
A380
BURDOUNS
EXETER RD.
EXETER
B3195
ROAD
GESTRIDGE
RD.
Five Lanes
LINDRIDGE
STRAP LA.
HELE RD.
Playing Field
Swim. Pool
MEADOWCROFT
FIRLEIGH RD.
FIRLEIGH ROAD
AVENUE
TEMPLER'S WY.
Playing Field
Teign School
PRINCESS RD.
LYNDALE RD.
NEW PARK RD.
BUTLAND RD.
CAPTAINS RD.
LANE
Leylane Cross
ROAD
Gestridge Cross
BROADWAY
GREENBANK AV.
WHITEWAY RD.
TWEENWAYS
ARCH COTTS.
Football Ground
Oakford Cross
Works
SORRELL CT.
ST. MICHAEL'S RD.
HOMERS LANE
NEWTON ROAD
Sch.
Lib.
OAKYMEAD PARK
Superstores
GREENHILL
A383
ROAD
KINGSTEIGNTON IND. EST.
RYDON IND. EST.
POTTERY RD.
Indoor Bowls Centre
RYDON
Rydon Quarry (Depot)
Prim. Sch.
Well Head
AVERY
RYDON ACRES
RYDON AV.
RYDON ESTATE
FOOTBALL LA.
Hall
LONGFORD
Play. Field
Wks.
STRAWBERRY TER.
CORONATION RD.
MOOR
HILL
GOLVERS
CROSSLEY
Higher Mills
CLIFFORD ST.
VICTORIA GS.
ORCHARD GS.
FORE STREET
CHURCH
BERRY LA.
BERRY MDW.
SANDPATH
GREENHILL RD.
KINGS CT.
WY.
Training Cen.
BLINDWELL
VICARAGE HILL
HONEYWELL
TEIGNMOUTH ROAD
Ware Cross
Penns Mount
KINGSTEIGNTON
HACKNEY LA.
HACKNEY
ASH RD.
WOODMERE
YEW TREE DR.
MAPLE CL.
ACACIA CL.
CHESTNUT DR.
THE MDWS.
LANE
HUMBER
NURSERY RD.
AVENUE
LONGFIELD
QUEENS
ABBOTSWOOD
HOLLAM WY.
FALKLAND DR.
WARECROFT RD.
COOMBESEND RD.
DARRAN RD.
DARRAN CL.
LONGFORD PK.
FAIRWATERS
Greyhound Track
Cycle Track
Playing Field
NEWTON ABBOT RACECOURSE
Hackney Canal Bridge
Hackney
Breakwater
Hackney Channel
Old Channel
RIVER TEIGN
Buckland Point
Newton Channel
Sewage Treatment Works
Tanks
Tanks
BESIGHEIM WAY
Subway
HACKNEY LA.
Teign

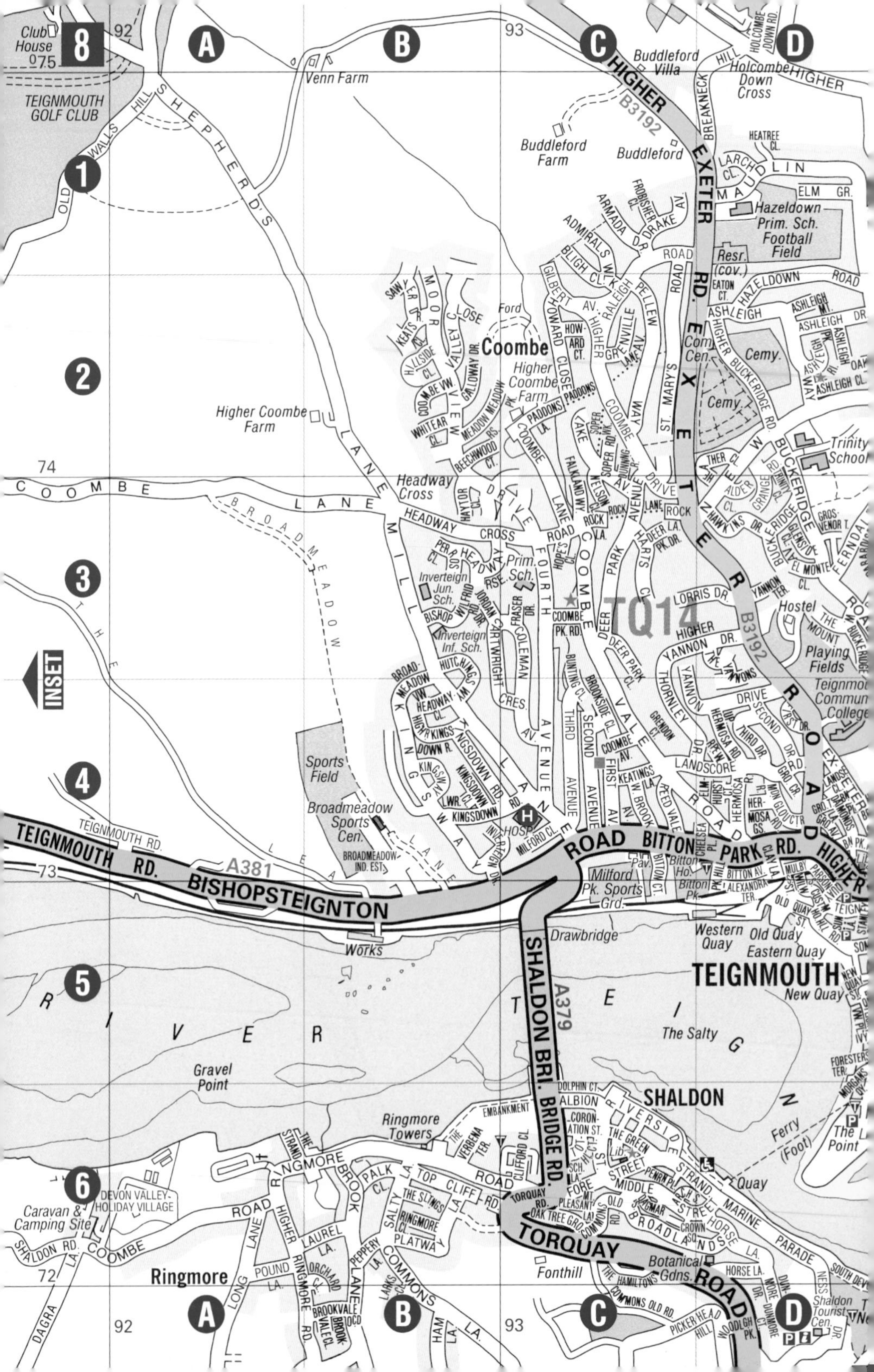

8
A
B
C
D
1
2
3
4
5
6
92
93
74
73
72
75
Club House
TEIGNMOUTH GOLF CLUB
OLD WALLS HILL
SHEPHERD'S LANE
Venn Farm
Buddleford Villa
Buddleford Farm
Buddleford
HIGHER EXETER RD.
B3192
BREAKNECK HILL
Holcombe Down Cross
HOLCOMBE DOWN RD.
HEATREE CL.
LARCH CL.
MAUDLIN
ELM GR.
Hazeldown Prim. Sch.
Football Field
Resr. (cov.)
EATON CT.
HAZELDOWN ROAD
ASHLEIGH
ASHLEIGH MT.
ASHLEIGH PK.
ASHLEIGH CL.
ASHLEIGH WAY
OAK
Cemy.
Com. Cen.
HIGHER BUCKERIDGE RD.
Trinity School
BUCKERIDGE
ALDER
GRANGE RD.
HAWKINS DR.
GROSVENOR T.
EL MONTE CL.
FERNDALE
FROBISHER CL.
ARMADA DR.
DRAKE AV.
ADMIRALS WK.
BLIGH CL.
RALEIGH
PELLEW ROAD
GILBERT AV.
HOWARD CLOSE
HOWARD CT.
GRENVILLE AV.
HIGHER COOMBE DR.
ST. MARY'S
Ford
Coombe
Higher Coombe Farm
PADDONS
PADDONS LA.
LAKE
SOPER RD.
SOPER WK.
COOMBE WAY
DRIVE
AVENUE
FALKLAND WY.
NELSON CL.
ROCK LA.
ROCK LANE
DEER LA.
DEER PK. DR.
HARTS CL.
SAWYER DR.
MOOR VIEW
KEATS CL.
HILLSIDE CL.
VALLEY CLOSE
GALLOWAY DR.
COOMBE VW.
WHITEAR CL.
MEADOW MEADOW
MEADOW RS.
BEECHWOOD CT.
COOMBE LA.
Higher Coombe Farm
COOMBE LANE
BROADMEADOW
Headway Cross
HEADWAY CROSS ROAD
HAYTOR CL.
DRIVE
PERROS CL.
HEADWAY RSE.
Prim. Sch.
Inverteign Jun. Sch.
Inverteign Inf. Sch.
BISHOP WILFRID RD.
JORDAN DR.
CARTWRIGHT CRES.
FRASER DR.
COLEMAN AV.
FOURTH AVENUE
COOMBE
COOMBE PK. RD.
DEER PARK
DEER PARK CL.
TQ14
LORRIS DR.
YANNON TER.
HIGHER YANNON DR.
YANNONS
THORNLEY DR.
Hostel
THE MOUNT
Playing Fields
BUCKERIDGE RD.
MILL LANE
HUTCHINGS WAY
BROADMEADOW VW.
HEADWAY CL.
KINGSWAY
KINGS DOWN R.
KINGSDOWN RD.
KINGSDOWN CL.
KINGSDOWN CR.
KINGSDOWN
HOSP.
H
MILFORD CL.
INVERTEIGN DR.
THIRD AVENUE
SECOND AVENUE
FIRST AV.
BUNTING CL.
BROOKSIDE CL.
COOMBE AV.
COOMBE VALE ROAD
GRENDON CT.
KEATINGS LA.
W. BROOK AV.
REED VALE
LANDSCORE
HERMOSA RD.
SECOND DR.
THIRD DR.
FIRST DR.
GRD. CR.
MON GLOU
EXETER ROAD
Teignmouth Community College
INSET
THE
Sports Field
Broadmeadow Sports Cen.
BROADMEADOW IND. EST.
LANE
LEA
TEIGNMOUTH RD.
TEIGNMOUTH RD.
A381
BISHOPSTEIGNTON
ROAD
BITTON PARK RD.
HIGHER
Milford Pk. Sports Grd.
Pav.
Bitton Ho.
Bitton Pk.
BITTON CT.
BITTON AV.
ALEXANDRA TER.
CHELSEA PL.
Works
Drawbridge
Western Quay
Old Quay
Eastern Quay
TEIGNMOUTH
New Quay
SHALDON BRI.
A379
RIVER TEIGN
Gravel Point
The Salty
FORESTERS TER.
SHALDON
DOLPHIN CT.
ALBION
RIVERSIDE
EMBANKMENT
CORONATION ST.
THE GREEN
Lib.
Ringmore Towers
THE VERBENA TER.
CLIFFORD CL.
BRIDGE RD.
FORE ST.
MIDDLE STREET
STRAND
MARINE PARADE
Quay
Ferry (Foot)
The Point
TORQUAY RD.
MT. PLEASANT
OAK TREE GRO.
COMMONS OLD RD.
CROWN SQ.
HORSE LA.
BROADLANDS
TORQUAY ROAD
Botanical Gdns.
Fonthill
THE HAMILTONS
COMMONS OLD RD.
PICKERHEAD HILL
WOODLEIGH PK.
DUNMORE DR.
NESS DR.
Shaldon Tourist Cen.
SOUTH DEVON
RINGMORE ROAD
THE STRAND
BROOK
PALK CL.
SALTY LA.
TOP CLIFF RD.
THE SLINGS
RINGMORE CL.
PLATWAY LA.
COMMONS LA.
PEPPERY LANE
LARKS CL.
HAM LA.
LAUREL LA.
ORCHARD CL.
HIGHER RINGMORE RD.
POUND LA.
LONG LANE
BROOKVALE
BROOK VALE CL.
DEVON VALLEY HOLIDAY VILLAGE
Caravan & Camping Site
SHALDON RD.
COOMBE
DAGRA LA.
Ringmore

9
HOLCOMBE
EX7
TQ14
Holcombe Covert
Higher Holcombe House
Higher Holcombe Farm
Court Farm
Manor Farm
Middle Holcombe House
Lower Holcombe Farm
East Down
Hole Head
The Parson and Clerk
Shag Rock
TEIGNMOUTH ROAD
DAWLISH ROAD
A379
Sprey Point
The Rowdens
ENGLISH CHANNEL
Teignmouth
Lido Pool
The Grand Pier
The Den
East Pole Sand
Lucette
ighthouse
Shaldon
dlife Trust
Ash Hill
Delamore
Shute Farm
BISHOPSTEIGNTON
Bishopsteignton House
Prim. Sch.
Lodge
High Winnard
Coles Barn House
Mus. & Comm. Cen.
Nursery
New Shute
NEWTON ROAD
A381
TEIGNMOUTH ROAD
INSET
E
F
G
H
1
2
3
4
5
6

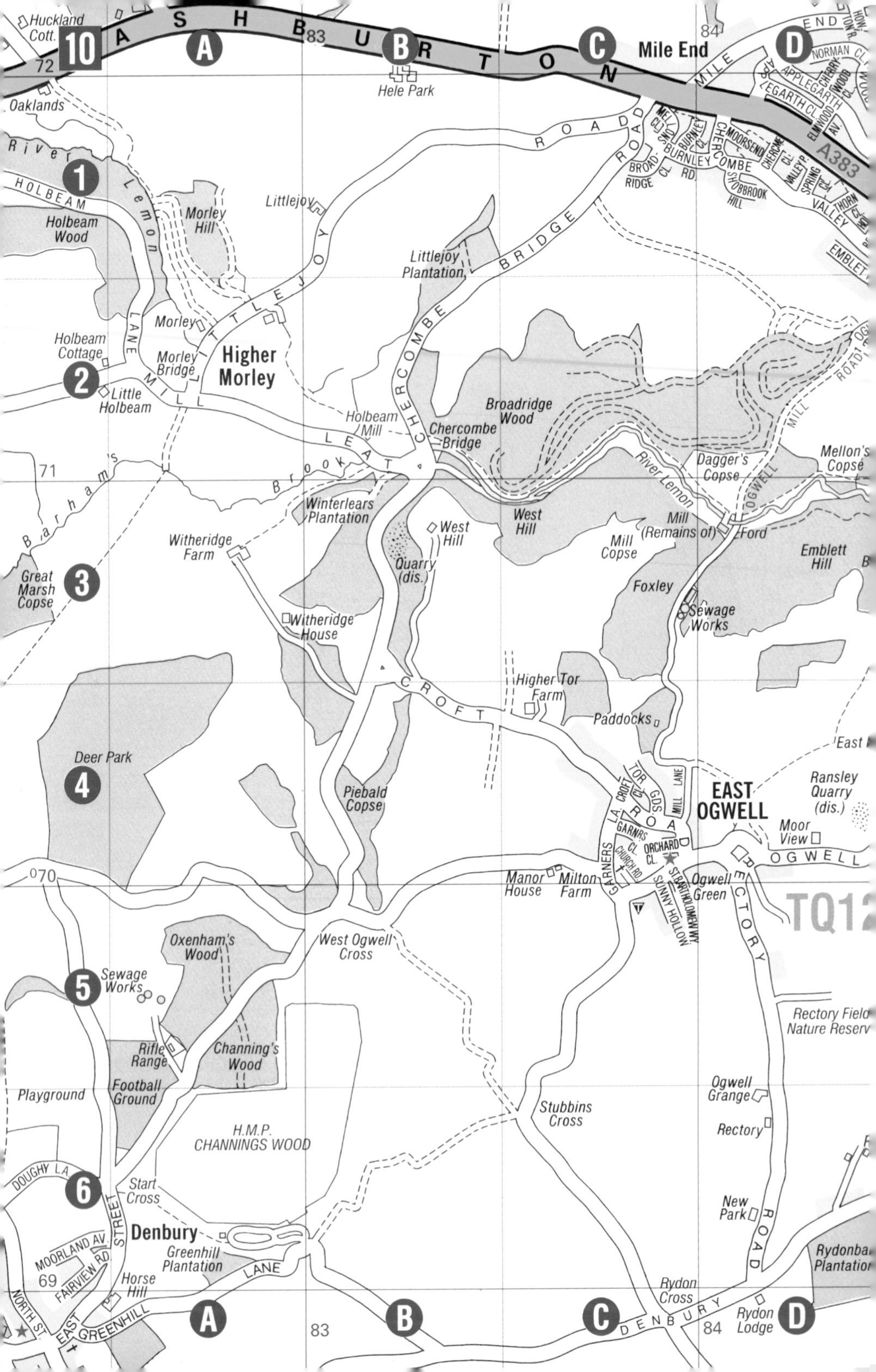
ASHBURTON ROAD
Mile End
Huckland Cott.
Oaklands
Hele Park
River Lemon
HOLBEAM LANE
Holbeam Wood
Morley Hill
Littlejoy
LITTLEJOY ROAD
Littlejoy Plantation
CHERCOMBE BRIDGE ROAD
Morley
Higher Morley
Morley Bridge
Holbeam Cottage
Little Holbeam
MILL LANE
Holbeam Mill
LEAT
Brook
Barham's
Chercombe Bridge
Broadridge Wood
Winterlears Plantation
West Hill
Witheridge Farm
Quarry (dis.)
Great Marsh Copse
Witheridge House
Dagger's Copse
Mill (Remains of)
Ford
Mill Copse
Foxley
Sewage Works
Emblett Hill
Mellon's Copse
OGWELL MILL ROAD
CROFT ROAD
Higher Tor Farm
Paddocks
Deer Park
Piebald Copse
EAST OGWELL
Ransley Quarry (dis.)
Moor View
OGWELL ROAD
RECTORY ROAD
Manor House
Milton Farm
GARNERS LA.
Ogwell Green
SUNNY HOLLOW
ORCHARD CL.
CHURCH RD.
TQ12
West Ogwell Cross
Oxenham's Wood
Sewage Works
Channing's Wood
Rifle Range
Football Ground
Playground
Rectory Field Nature Reserve
Ogwell Grange
Rectory
Stubbins Cross
H.M.P. CHANNINGS WOOD
DOUGHY LA.
Start Cross
STREET
Denbury
MOORLAND AV.
FAIRVIEW RD.
Greenhill Plantation
Horse Hill
LANE
GREENHILL
EAST
NORTH ST.
New Park
Rydon Cross
DENBURY ROAD
Rydon Lodge
Rydonbar Plantation
MILE END
NORMAN CL.
APPLEGARTH CL.
CHERRY WOOD CL.
ELMWOOD AV.
BURNLEY CL.
BURNLEY RD.
BROADRIDGE CL.
CHERCOMBE VALLEY
MOORSEND
SHOBBROOK HILL
VALLEY P.
SPRING CL.
THORN CL.
A383
EMBLETT
A B C D
1 2 3 4 5 6
72 71 070 69
83 84

Gaze
Memorial
Sandford Orleigh
Nature Reserve
Depot
Kingsteignton Road Bridge
6
JETTY
MARSH
E
F
G
H
1
2
3
4
5
6
Castle Dyke
COOMBESHEAD
Coombeshead College
Prim. Sch.
Play. Flds.
EXETER ROAD
KNOWLES HILL
Knowles Hill School
Dyrons Leisure Cen.
ROAD
A383
NEWTON RD.
Whitelake
THE AVENUE
Works
S. Devon Cricket Grd.
KINGSTEIGNTON RD.
B3195
Osborne Park
HALCYON RD.
College
Prim. Sch.
BROADLANDS
Playground
Lib.
Abbotsbury
EAST ST.
TORQUAY RD.
A381
STATION ROAD
Courtenay Park
Offs.
Industrial Est.
Fort
Berry's Wood
Berry's Wood (N.T.)
River Lemon
Baker's Park
Bradley Manor (N.T.)
Tennis Courts
Nursery
Newton Abbot Hosp.
Highwood House
NEWTON ABBOT
Wolborough Hill Sch.
Powsey Moor
Lang's Copse (N.T.)
WOLBOROUGH
WOLBOROUGH ST.
ROAD
Ten. Cts.
Forde Park
12
Recreation Ground
COLLEGE
COACH
Nursery
Wolborough Barton
Quarry (dis.)
Hosp.
Prim. Sch.
Cemy.
Ogwell Cross
Decoy Lake
Decoy Recreation Area
Playing Fields
DECOY COUNTRY PARK
Magazine Pond
Decoy Brake
Rifle Range (dis.)
DECOY INDUSTRIAL ESTATE
Quarry (dis.)
Cave
Depot
Conitor Copse
Conitor
Higher Langford
Crystalwood
Goldmore
STONEMAN'S LANE
FIRESTONE
DENBURY
Rydonball Cross
Higherdown Gardens
Prickly Ball Farm (Hedgehog Hospital)
Oldbarn Cross
Abbotskerswell Cross
The Old Cider Works
TOTNES
A381
ABBOTSKERSWELL
Hennaborough
PRIORY ROAD
The Mallands
St. Augustine's Priory
14
VICARAGE
Vicarage
Prim. Sch.
285
86
72
71
70
69

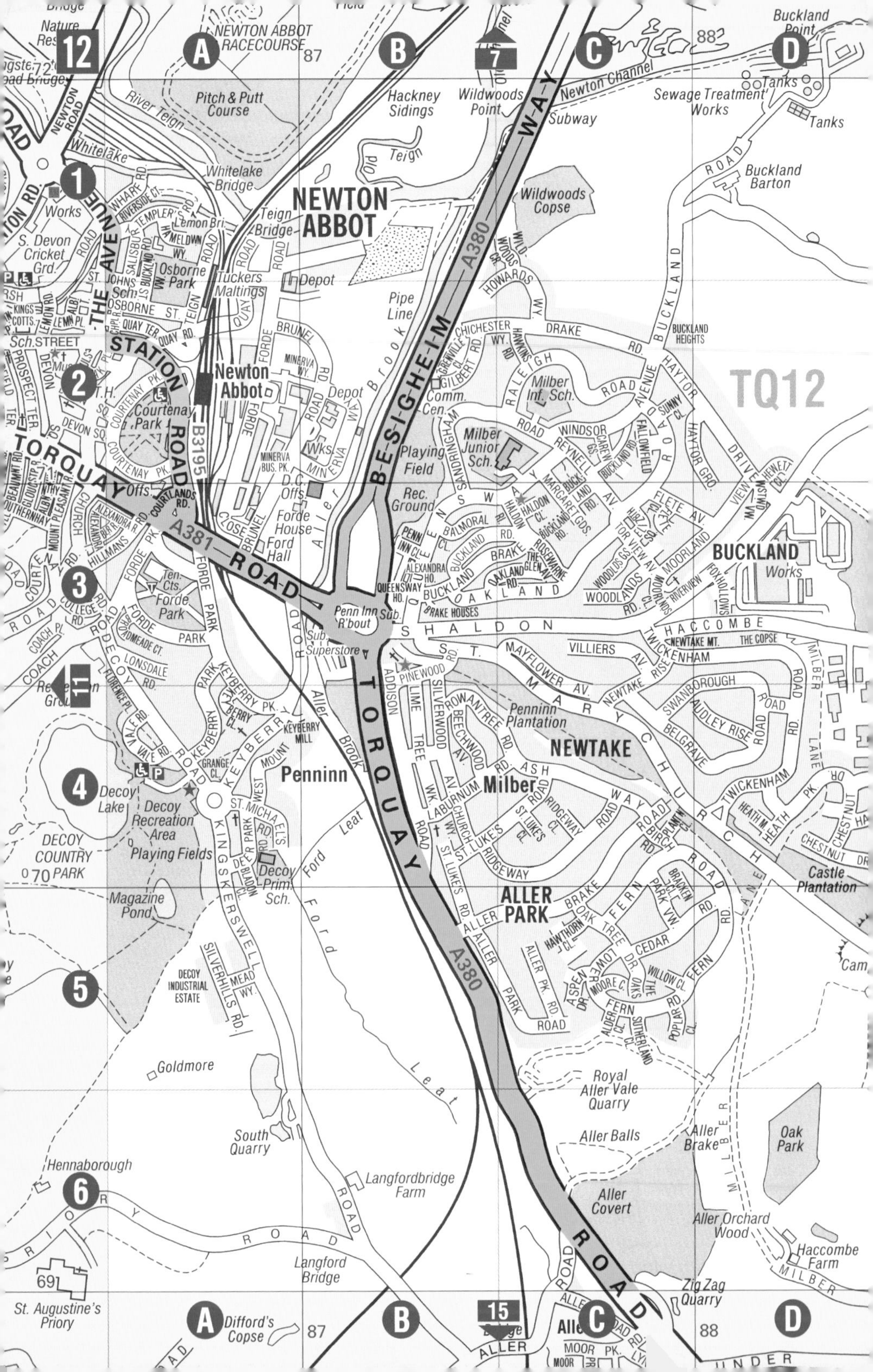
12
A
B
C
D
7
NEWTON ABBOT RACECOURSE
87
88
Buckland Point
Pitch & Putt Course
River Teign
Hackney Sidings
Wildwoods Point
Newton Channel
Sewage Treatment Works
Tanks
Subway
Whitelake
Whitelake Bridge
NEWTON ROAD
Teign
NEWTON ABBOT
Teign Bridge
Wildwoods Copse
Buckland Barton
Works
S. Devon Cricket Grd.
THE AVENUE
Osborne Park
Tuckers Maltings
Depot
Pipe Line
STATION ROAD
Newton Abbot
B3195
BESIGHEIM WAY
A380
TQ12
BUCKLAND HEIGHTS
Milber Inf. Sch.
Milber Junior Sch.
Comm. Cen.
Playing Field
Rec. Ground
Courtenay Park
TORQUAY ROAD
A381
Minerva Bus. Pk.
D.C. Offs.
Forde House
Ford Hall
Penn Inn R'bout
Superstore
BUCKLAND
SHALDON ROAD
HACCOMBE
TWICKENHAM
Forde Park
Ten. Cts.
11
Keyberry Mill
Penninn Plantation
NEWTAKE
Penninn
Milber
Decoy Lake
Decoy Recreation Area
Playing Fields
DECOY COUNTRY PARK
70
Decoy Prim. Sch.
Castle Plantation
Magazine Pond
ALLER PARK
Decoy Industrial Estate
Goldmore
Royal Aller Vale Quarry
South Quarry
Aller Balls
Aller Brake
Oak Park
Hennaborough
Langfordbridge Farm
Aller Covert
Aller Orchard Wood
PRIORY ROAD
Hackney Farm
Haccombe Farm
Langford Bridge
69
St. Augustine's Priory
Zig Zag Quarry
Difford's Copse
15
1
2
3
4
5
6

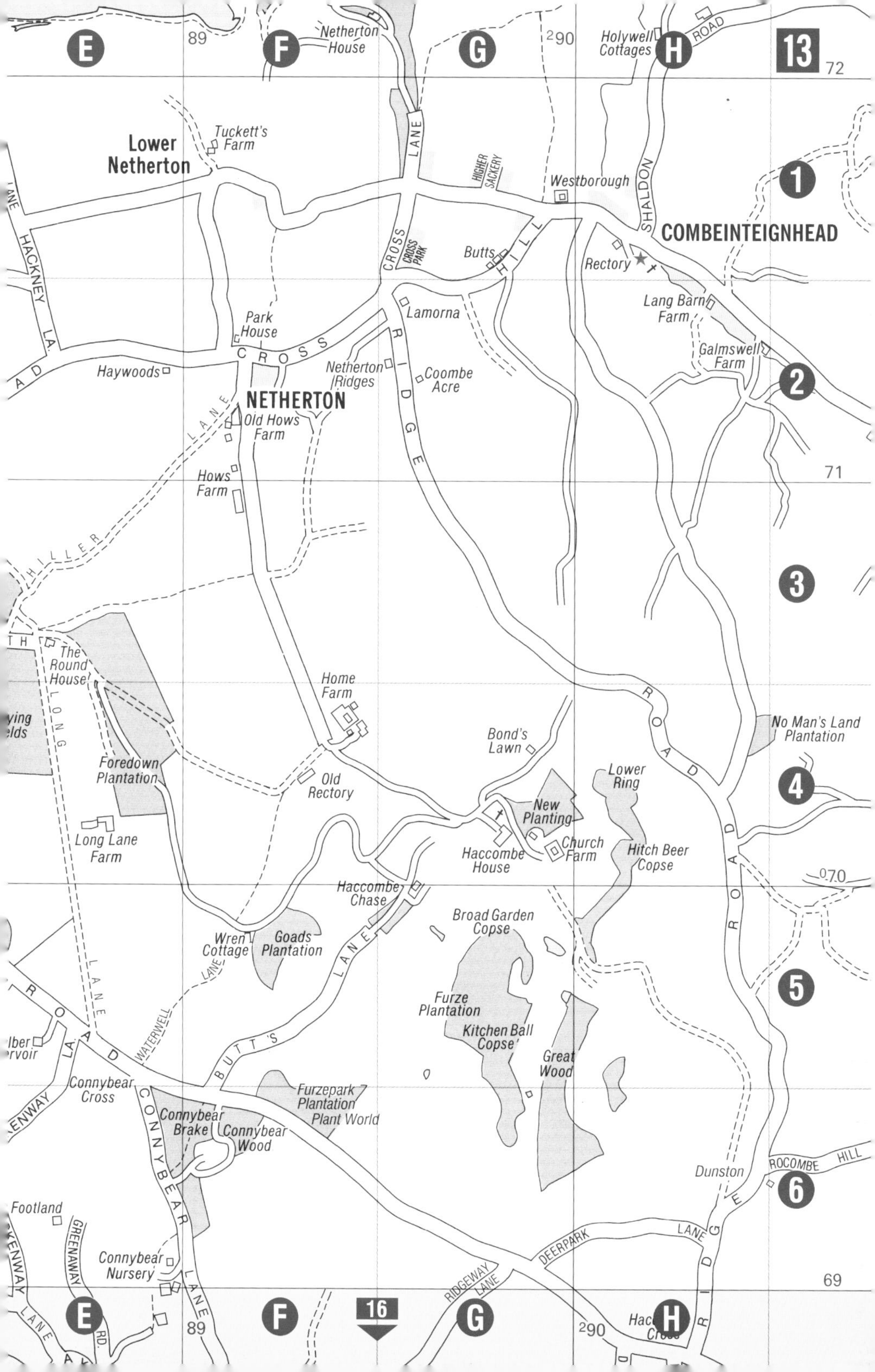
E
F
G
H
89
290
72
71
070
69
1
2
3
4
5
6
Netherton House
Holywell Cottages
ROAD
Lower Netherton
Tuckett's Farm
LANE
HIGHER SACKERY
Westborough
SHALDON
COMBEINTEIGNHEAD
HACKNEY LA.
CROSS
CROSS PARK
Butts
HILL
Rectory
Lang Barn Farm
Lamorna
Park House
CROSS
Galmswell Farm
Haywoods
Netherton Ridges
Coombe Acre
RIDGE
NETHERTON
LANE
Old Hows Farm
Hows Farm
HILLER
The Round House
LONG
Home Farm
ROAD
No Man's Land Plantation
Bond's Lawn
Lower Ring
Foredown Plantation
Old Rectory
New Planting
Long Lane Farm
Haccombe House
Church Farm
Hitch Beer Copse
Haccombe Chase
Broad Garden Copse
Wren Cottage
Goads Plantation
LANE
LANE
ROAD
Furze Plantation
Kitchen Ball Copse
WATERWELL
BUTT'S
Great Wood
Connybear Cross
Furzepark Plantation
Plant World
Connybear Brake
Connybear Wood
CONNYBEAR
Dunston
ROCOMBE HILL
Footland
GREENAWAY
DEERPARK
LANE
RIDGE
Connybear Nursery
LANE
RIDGEWAY LANE
16
RD.

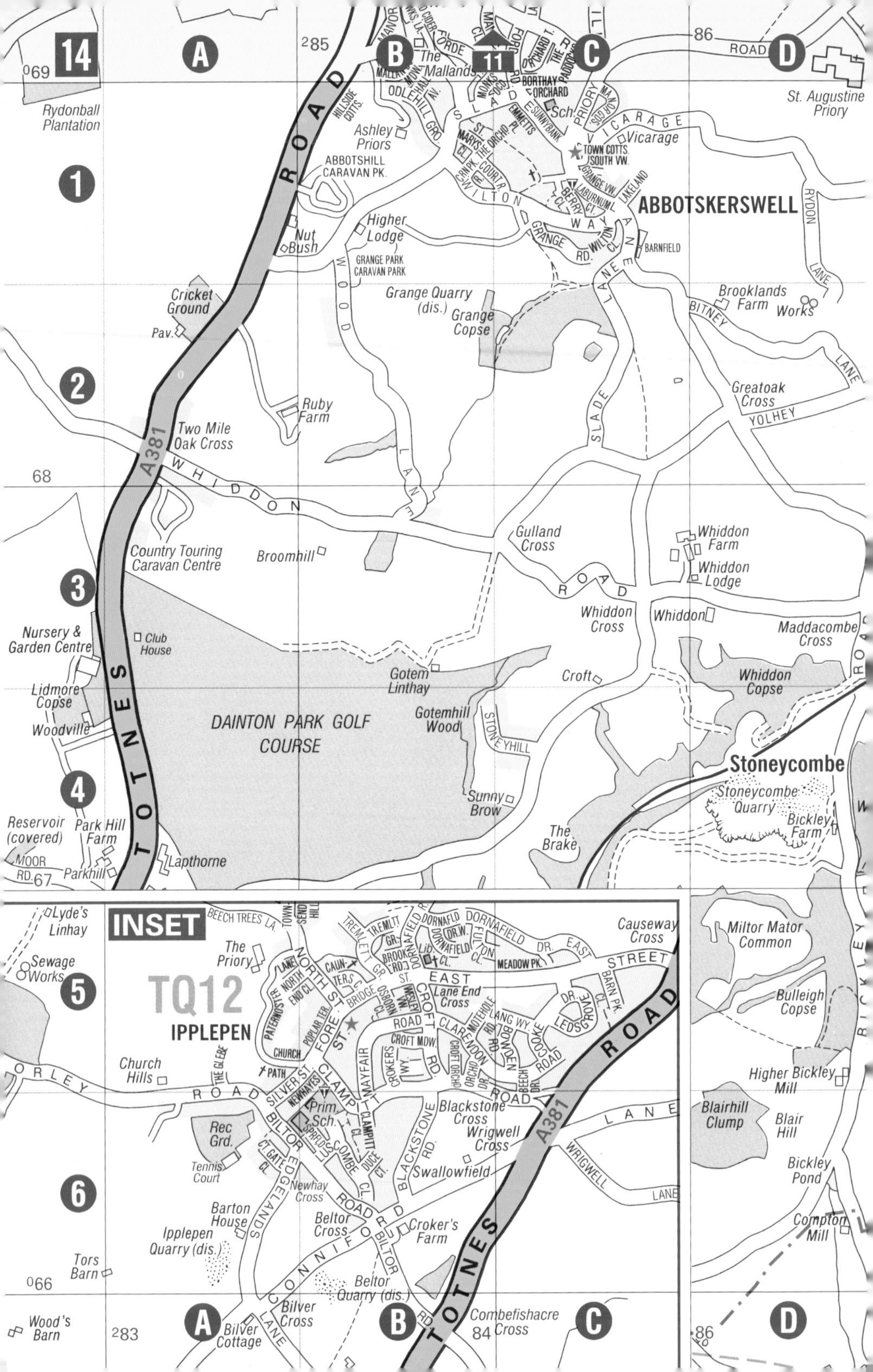

A
B
C
D
11
Rydonball Plantation
St. Augustine Priory
The Mallands
Ashley Priors
ABBOTSHILL CARAVAN PK.
Vicarage
ABBOTSKERSWELL
Higher Lodge
Nut Bush
GRANGE PARK CARAVAN PARK
BARNFIELD
Grange Quarry (dis.)
Grange Copse
Brooklands Farm
Works
Cricket Ground
Pav.
Ruby Farm
Greatoak Cross
Two Mile Oak Cross
A381
WHIDDON
Gulland Cross
Whiddon Farm
Whiddon Lodge
Country Touring Caravan Centre
Broomhill
Whiddon Cross
Whiddon
Maddacombe Cross
Nursery & Garden Centre
Club House
Gotem Linthay
Croft
Whiddon Copse
Lidmore Copse
Woodville
DAINTON PARK GOLF COURSE
Gotemhill Wood
STONEYHILL
Stoneycombe
Stoneycombe Quarry
Sunny Brow
The Brake
Bickley Farm
Reservoir (covered)
Park Hill Farm
Lapthorne
Parkhill
TOTNES ROAD
INSET
Lyde's Linhay
Sewage Works
The Priory
TQ12
IPPLEPEN
Causeway Cross
EAST STREET
Lane End Cross
Miltor Mator Common
Bulleigh Copse
Church Hills
Higher Bickley Mill
Blackstone Cross
Wrigwell Cross
Blairhill Clump
Blair Hill
Rec Grd.
Prim. Sch.
Tennis Court
Swallowfield
Bickley Pond
Newhay Cross
Barton House
Beltor Cross
Croker's Farm
Compton Mill
Ipplepen Quarry (dis.)
Tors Barn
Beltor Quarry (dis.)
Bilver Cross
Combefishacre Cross
Wood's Barn
Bilver Cottage

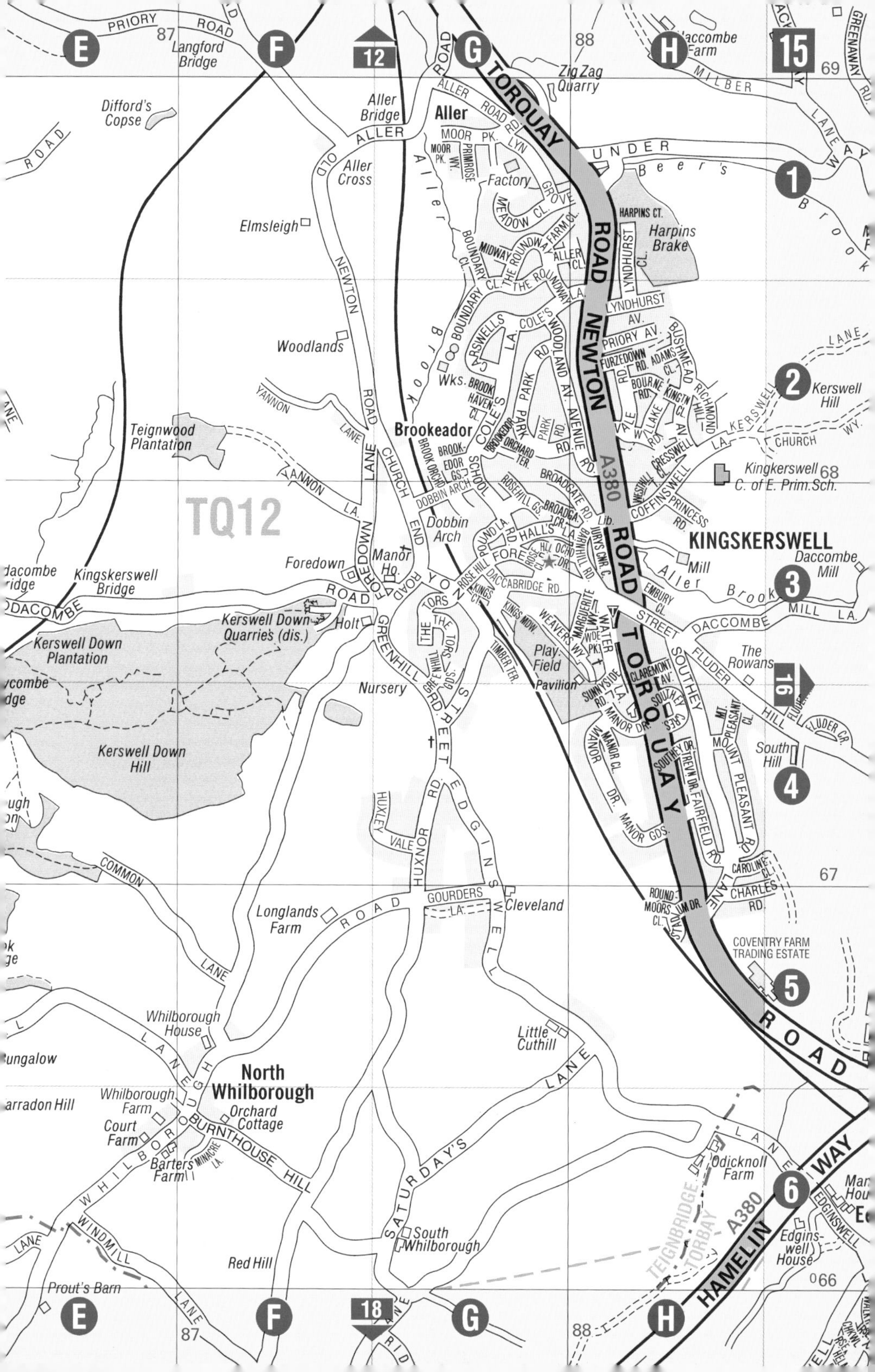
15
12
18
16
E
F
G
H
1
2
3
4
5
6
87
88
69
68
67
66
TQ12
PRIORY ROAD
Langford Bridge
Daccombe Farm
Zig Zag Quarry
MILBER
GREENAWAY RD.
LANE WAY
Difford's Copse
Aller Bridge
Aller
ALLER ROAD
TORQUAY
UNDER
Beer's Brook
Aller Cross
OLD NEWTON ROAD
MOOR PK.
PRIMROSE
LYN GROVE
Factory
MEADOW CL.
FARM CL.
HARPINS CT.
Harpins Brake
LYNDHURST CL.
Elmsleigh
BOUNDARY CL.
MIDWAY
THE ROUNDWAY
ALLER CL.
LYNDHURST AV.
PRIORY AV.
BUSHMEAD
NEWTON
ROAD
Woodlands
CARSWELLS
COLE'S LA.
WOODLAND AV.
PARK RD.
FURZEDOWN RD.
ADAMS CL.
BOURNE RD.
KINGTN CL.
RICHMOND HILL
Kerswell Hill
Wks.
BROOK HAVEN CL.
YANNON LANE
Teignwood Plantation
Brookeador
BROOKEADOR
ORCHARD TER.
PARK RD.
AVENUE RD.
VALE RD.
WILLAKE RD.
CRESSWELL CL.
KERSWELL LA.
CHURCH WY.
Kingkerswell C. of E. Prim.Sch.
YANNON LA.
LANE
CHURCH END
SCHOOL
DOBBIN ARCH
ROSEHILL GS.
BROADGATE RD.
A380
WESTHILL
COFFINSWELL
PRINCESS RD.
Dobbin Arch
HALL'S LA.
POUND LA.
BARNHILL RD.
JURYS CNR. C.
Lib.
KINGSKERSWELL
Foredown
Manor Ho.
FORE
ROSE HILL
ORCHD DR.
Mill
Aller Brook
Daccombe Mill
Kingskerswell Bridge
ROAD
FOREDOWN
YON
DACCABRIDGE RD.
EMBURY CL.
DACCOMBE
DACCOMBE MILL LA.
Kerswell Down Quarries (dis.)
Holt
THE TORS
KINGS MDW.
WEAVERS WY.
MARGUERITE
WATER
STREET
SOUTHEY
FLUDER
The Rowans
Kerswell Down Plantation
GREENHILL
Play Field
Pavilion
CLAREMONT AV.
SUNNYSIDE RD.
TIMBER TER.
Nursery
MANOR DR.
SOUTHEY CRES.
MT. PLEASANT CL.
FLUDER HILL
FLUDER CR.
Kerswell Down Hill
STREET
MANOR CL.
SOUTHEY DR.
TREVIN DR.
MOUNT PLEASANT RD.
South Hill
HUXLEY VALE
HUXNOR RD.
EDGINSWELL
MANOR GDS.
FAIRFIELD RD.
CAROLINE CL.
COMMON
CHARLES RD.
GOURDERS LA.
Cleveland
ROUND MOORS CL.
STADIUM DR.
Longlands Farm
ROAD
COVENTRY FARM TRADING ESTATE
LANE
Whilborough House
Little Cuthill
LANE
North Whilborough
Whilborough Farm
Orchard Cottage
Court Farm
BURNTHOUSE HILL
SATURDAY'S
Barters Farm
MINACRE LA.
Odicknoll Farm
WAY
HAMELIN
WHILBOROUGH
WINDMILL LANE
South Whilborough
TEIGNBRIDGE
TORBAY
Edginswell House
Red Hill
Prout's Barn
LANE
RIDGE

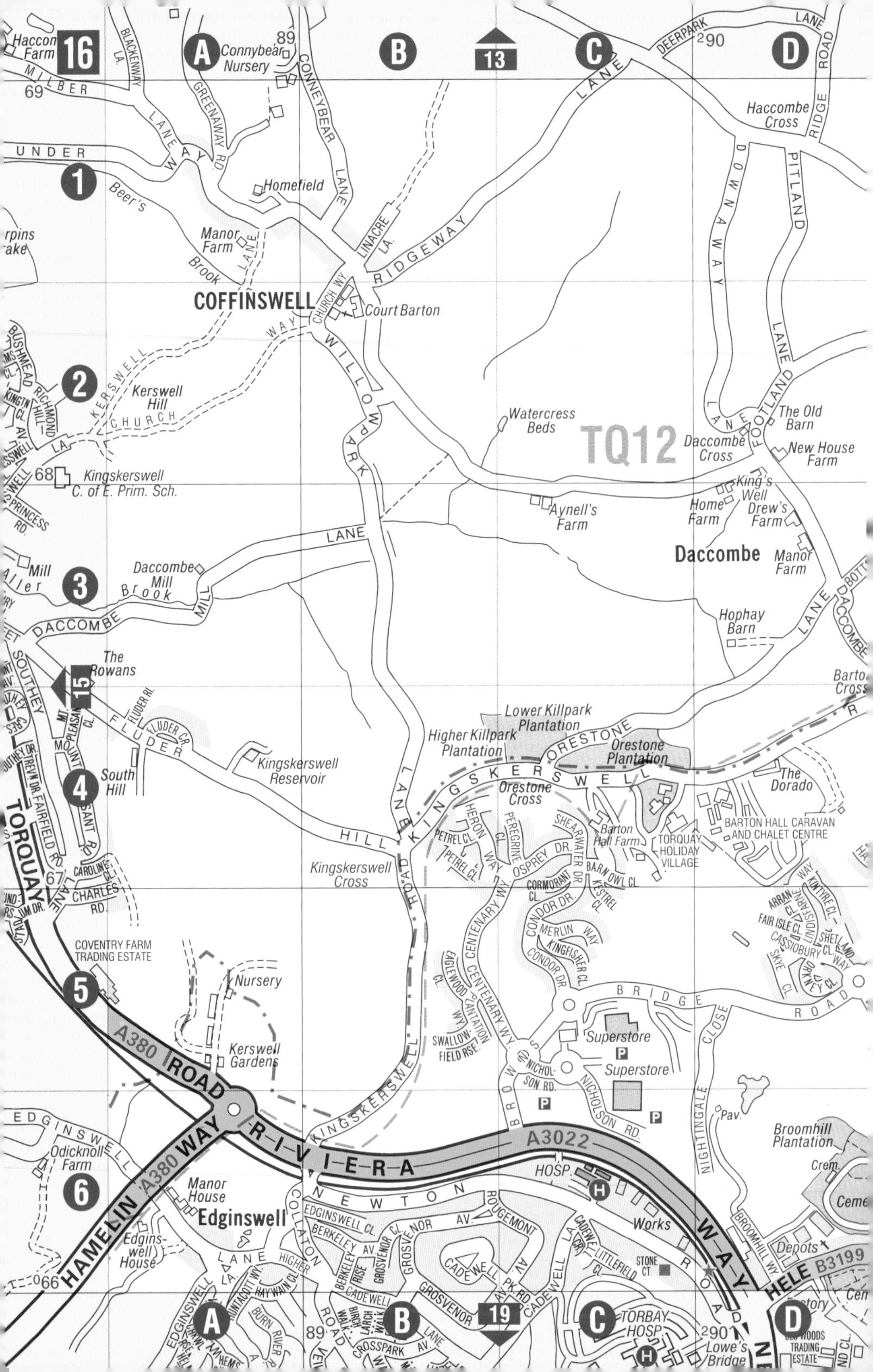

13
A
B
C
D
1
2
3
4
5
6
15
19
COFFINSWELL
Daccombe
Edginswell
TQ12
Haccombe Farm
Connybear Nursery
Homefield
Manor Farm
Court Barton
Kerswell Hill
Kingskerswell C. of E. Prim. Sch.
Haccombe Cross
The Old Barn
New House Farm
Watercress Beds
Daccombe Cross
King's Well
Home Farm
Drew's Farm
Aynell's Farm
Manor Farm
Hophay Barn
Daccombe Mill
The Rowans
South Hill
Kingskerswell Reservoir
Lower Killpark Plantation
Higher Killpark Plantation
Orestone Plantation
Orestone Cross
The Dorado
Barton Hall Farm
TORQUAY HOLIDAY VILLAGE
BARTON HALL CARAVAN AND CHALET CENTRE
Kingskerswell Cross
COVENTRY FARM TRADING ESTATE
Nursery
Kerswell Gardens
Superstore
Superstore
Odicknoll Farm
Manor House
Edgins-well House
HOSP.
Works
STONE CT.
Broomhill Plantation
Crem.
Depots
TORBAY HOSP.
Lowe's Bridge
Factory
OLD WOODS TRADING ESTATE
Pav.
A380 ROAD
RIVIERA WAY
A3022
HAMELIN WAY
A380
HELE B3199
MILBER
UNDER
LANE WAY
GREENAWAY RD.
BLACKENWAY LA.
CONNEYBEAR LANE
LINACRE LA.
RIDGEWAY
CHURCH WY.
WILLOW PARK
LANE
DEERPARK
LANE
RIDGE ROAD
DOWNAWAY LANE
PITLAND LANE
FOOTLAND LANE
Beer's Brook
KERSWELL CHURCH LA.
DACCOMBE MILL LANE
Aller Brook
DACCOMBE HILL
FLUDER
FLUDER CR.
MT. PLEASANT CL.
SOUTHEY
MOUNT PLEASANT RD.
FAIRFIELD RD.
CAROLINE CL.
CHARLES RD.
LANE
TORQUAY
LANE ROAD
KINGSKERSWELL ROAD
ORESTONE
KINGSKERSWELL
HERON WAY
PETREL CL.
PEREGRINE CL.
OSPREY DR.
SHEARWATER DR.
BARN OWL CL.
CORMORANT CL.
KESTREL CL.
CENTENARY WY.
CONDOR DR.
MERLIN WAY
KINGFISHER CL.
EAGLEWOOD CL.
PLANTATION WY.
SWALLOWFIELD RSE.
BROWNS BRIDGE ROAD
NICHOLSON RD.
CLOSE
NIGHTINGALE
ARRAN CL.
FAIR ISLE CL.
KINTYRE CL.
LINDISFARNE WAY
SHETLAND CL.
CASSIOBURY WAY
SKYE CL.
ORKNEY CL.
EDGINSWELL
NEWTON ROAD
COLLATON ROAD
EDGINSWELL CL.
BERKELEY AV.
BERKELEY RISE
GROSVENOR AV.
GROSVENOR CL.
ROUGEMONT AV.
CADEWELL PK. RD.
CADEWELL LA.
CADEWELL CR.
LITTLEFIELD CL.
BROOMHILL WY.
EDGINSWELL LANE
HIGHER
HUNTACOTT WY.
HAYWAIN CL.
BURN RIVER
CADEWELL
BIRCH WALK
LARCH WALK
CROSSPARK AV.
DACCOMBE
Barton Cross
69
89
290
68
67
66
89
290

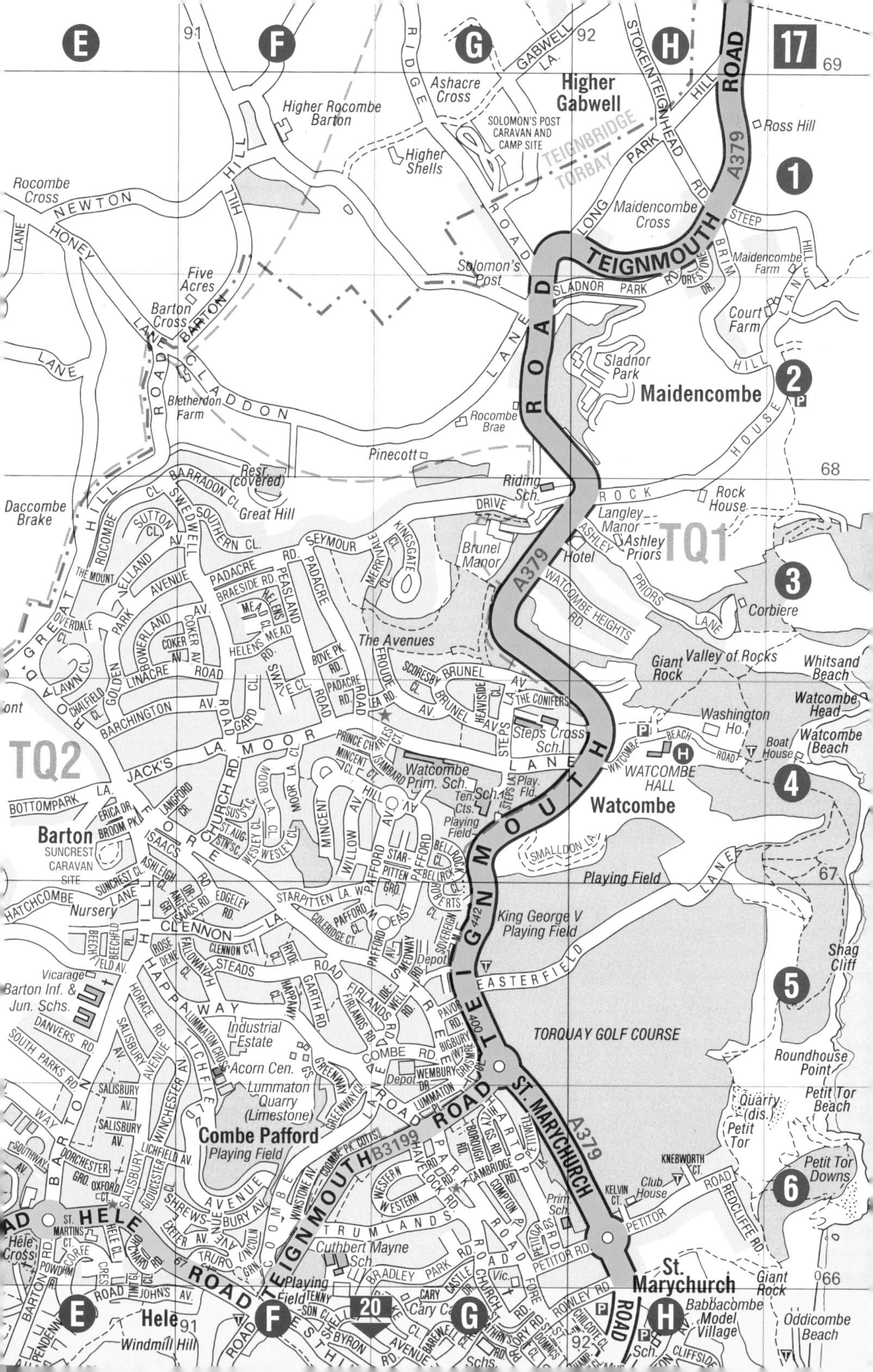

Higher Gabwell
Higher Rocombe Barton
Ashacre Cross
Higher Shells
SOLOMON'S POST CARAVAN AND CAMP SITE
TEIGNBRIDGE
TORBAY
Ross Hill
Rocombe Cross
Maidencombe Cross
Maidencombe Farm
Court Farm
Five Acres
Barton Cross
Solomon's Post
Sladnor Park
Maidencombe
Bletherdon Farm
Rocombe Brae
Pinecott
Resr. (covered)
Great Hill
Riding Sch.
Rock House
Daccombe Brake
Langley Manor
Ashley Priors
Hotel
TQ1
Brunel Manor
Corbiere
The Avenues
Giant Rock
Valley of Rocks
Whitsand Beach
Watcombe Head
Watcombe Beach
Washington Ho.
Boat House
Steps Cross Sch.
TQ2
Watcombe Prim. Sch.
WATCOMBE HALL
Watcombe
Barton
SUNCREST CARAVAN SITE
Playing Field
Nursery
King George V Playing Field
Shag Cliff
Vicarage
Barton Inf. & Jun. Schs.
TORQUAY GOLF COURSE
Industrial Estate
Acorn Cen.
Lummaton Quarry (Limestone)
Roundhouse Point
Petit Tor Beach
Quarry (dis.)
Petit Tor
Combe Pafford
Playing Field
Petit Tor Downs
Club House
Prim. Sch.
Hele Cross
Cuthbert Mayne Sch.
Playing Field
St. Marychurch
Giant Rock
Babbacombe Model Village
Hele
Windmill Hill
Cary Ca
Oddicombe Beach
TEIGNMOUTH ROAD
ST. MARYCHURCH ROAD
HELE ROAD
A379
B3199
20
E F G H
1 2 3 4 5 6
91 92 69 68 67 66

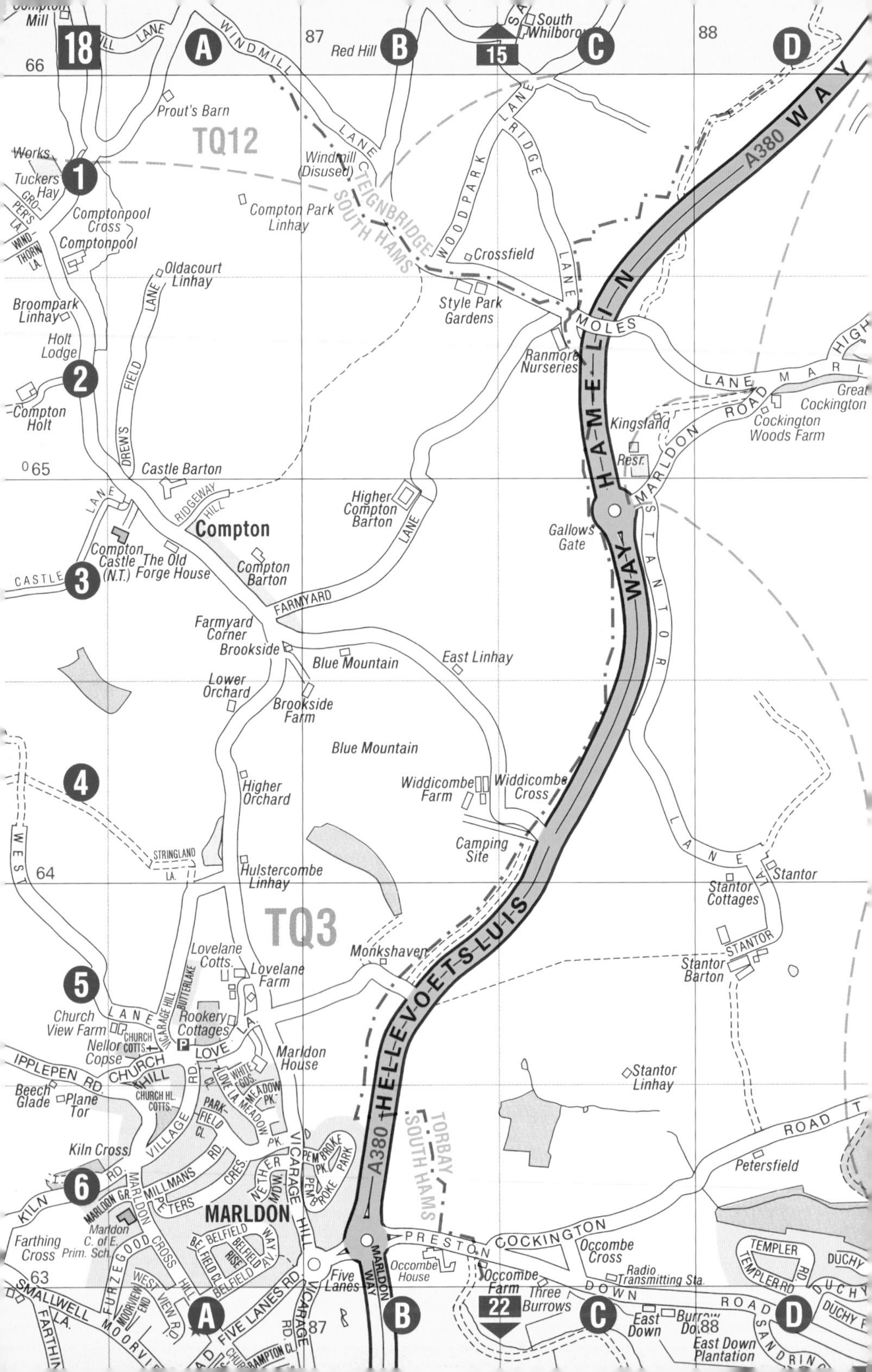

18
15
22
A
B
C
D
1
2
3
4
5
6
87
88
66
65
64
63
TQ12
TQ3
Compton
MARLDON
Red Hill
South Whilborough
Prout's Barn
Works
Tuckers Hay
Comptonpool Cross
Comptonpool
Windmill (Disused)
Compton Park Linhay
TEIGNBRIDGE
SOUTH HAMS
Oldacourt Linhay
Crossfield
Style Park Gardens
Broompark Linhay
Holt Lodge
Compton Holt
Ranmore Nurseries
Kingsland
Resr.
Great Cockington
Cockington Woods Farm
Castle Barton
Higher Compton Barton
Gallows Gate
Compton Castle (N.T.)
The Old Forge House
Compton Barton
Farmyard Corner
Brookside
Blue Mountain
East Linhay
Lower Orchard
Brookside Farm
Widdicombe Farm
Widdicombe Cross
Higher Orchard
Camping Site
Hulstercombe Linhay
Stantor
Stantor Cottages
Monkshaven
Lovelane Cotts.
Lovelane Farm
Stantor Barton
Church View Farm
Rookery Cottages
Nellor Copse
Marldon House
Stantor Linhay
Beech Glade
Plane Tor
Kiln Cross
Petersfield
Farthing Cross
Marldon C. of E. Prim. Sch.
Five Lanes
Occombe House
Occombe Cross
Radio Transmitting Sta.
Occombe Farm
Three Burrows
East Down
Burrow Down
East Down Plantation
TORBAY
SOUTH HAMS
A380 WAY
HAMELIN WAY
A380 HELLEVOETSLUIS WAY
WINDMILL LANE
WOODPARK LANE
RIDGE LANE
MOLES LANE
MARLDON ROAD
STANTOR LANE
DREW'S FIELD LANE
RIDGEWAY HILL
FARMYARD LANE
CASTLE LANE
STRINGLAND LA.
WEST
BUTTERLAKE
VICARAGE HILL
LOVE LA.
CHURCH HILL
IPPLEPEN RD.
CHURCH COTTS.
CHURCH HL. COTTS.
VILLAGE RD.
WHITE GDS.
MEADOW PK.
LOVE LA. MEADOW
PARK FIELD CL.
MILLMANS RD.
CRES.
NETHER MDW.
PEMBROKE PK.
PEMBROKE PARK
KILN RD.
MARLDON GR.
PETERS CRES.
MARLDON CROSS HILL
FURZEGOOD
BELFIELD RD.
BELFIELD RISE
BELFIELD AV.
BELFIELD WAY
WEST VIEW RD.
MOORVIEW END
SMALLWELL LA.
FARTHING LA.
MOORVIEW
FIVE LANES RD.
VICARAGE RD.
MARLDON WAY
BAMPTON CL.
PRESTON DOWN ROAD
COCKINGTON
TEMPLER RD.
DUCHY
SANDRINGHAM

E
F
G
H
16
19
20
23
1
2
3
4
5
6
89
290
66
65
64
63
TQ2
TQ1
Works
Stone Ct.
Roomhill Wy.
Hele
Road
Cemetery
Factory
Torbay Hospital
Lowe's Bridge
Medical Centre
Old Woods Trading Estate
Woodland Cl.
Woodland Rd.
Newton
Bus Depot
Regent Cl.
Audley
Pendennis
Fairfield Rd.
Charlotte Cl.
Kirkstead Cl.
Torquay Comm. Coll.
Playing Fields
Cricketfield Rd.
Torre C. of E. Prim. Sch.
Parkhurst
A3022
Resr. (covered)
Chapel Hill
St. Michael's Chapel
Hosp.
Rooklands Av.
Coll.
Oakhill
Higher
Lane La.
Berkeley Av.
Berkeley Rise
Grosvenor Cl.
Grosvenor Av.
Cadewell
Cadewell La.
Haywain Cl.
Huntacott Wy.
Burn River Ri.
Collaton Rd.
Crosspark Av.
Wallace Av.
Hazel
Maple Wk.
Prim. Sch.
Culvery Grn.
Glebeland
Culm Cl.
Falmouth Cl.
Water La.
Banbury Pk.
Oak Pk. Av.
Cuckoo Pit Farm
Shiphay Park Road
Lloyd Av.
Lloyd Avenue
Summerfield Rd.
Shiphay
Shiphay Lane
Shiphay Av.
Kenneth
Dart
Yealm
Dairy Hill
Stanbury Rd.
Otter Rd.
Tavy Av.
Torridge Av.
Severn Rd.
Plym Cl.
Avon Rd.
Tamar Avenue
Torridge
Road
Queensway Cl.
Mar Lowe Cl.
Torquay Grammer Sch. For Boys
Torquay Grammar Sch. For Girls Playing Fld.
Queensway R.C. Prim. Sch.
Shiphay Manor Drive
Shiphay Manor
Playing Field
Heywood Cl.
Rainbow Ct.
Fletcher Cl.
Wordsworth Cl.
Playing Fields
Sherwell Valley Prim. Sch.
Ferndale Rd.
Burleigh Rd.
Courtland
Cornacre Road
Cornacre Rd.
Cockington Lane
Hawkins Av.
Nut
Bush
Little Cockington Wood
Armada Park
Frobisher Grn.
Frobisher Grn.
Sherwell
Raleigh
Davis Av.
Oxenham Grn.
Grenville
Arden Dr.
Shakespeare Cl.
Beaumont Cl.
Ben Jonson Cl.
Shiphay Plantn.
Torre
The Rainbow
Crownhill Rise
Crownhill Pk.
Hospice
Howard Cl.
Gilbert Cl.
St. Peters Cl.
Staddons
Lea La.
Weeksland Rd.
Highland Cl.
Highland
Valley
Horse Barton
Cockington
Court
Road
Fruit Farm Copse
Blindwylle Rd.
Victoria Park
Sherwell Rise Sth.
Reeves Road
Sherwell Pk. Rd.
Mallock Road
Pimuir Av.
Torre
Lansdowne Rd.
Elizabeth Ct.
Mill
Rowdens
Bridge
Bexley La.
Burridge Av.
Sherwell
Ashfield
Marcombe Rd.
Ruckamore Rd.
Ashfield Gs.
Devon Learning Resource Cen.
Innerbrook Rd.
Sanford Rd.
Millbrook Pk. Rd.
Rosery Rd.
Goshen Rd.
Sch.
Playing Field
Bampflyde
Falkland
Rathmore Rd.
Rosery Grange
Brambie Cl.
Thorne Park
Meadow Farm
Foxhole Rd.
Boundary Rd.
Huxtable Hill
Almhouses
Cockington Country Pk. Visitor Cen.
Loxbury Rise
Ridgefield
Herbert Rd.
Greenway
Chelston
Rousdown
Cockington Court
Pav.
Cockington Country Park
Vicarage
Forgewy Cl.
St. Matthew's Road
Walnut
Walnut La.
Brunel M.
Solsbro
Two Parks
Chelston Rd.
St. Agnes La.
Torquay
Church Wood
Cockington
Cockington Forge
Seaway
Rawlyn Rd.
Brooklands
Lanscombe
Lodge
Warren Barn
Hellinghay Plantation
Thornhill Brake
Meadow Rd.
Seaway Cl.
Monterey Cl.
Hennapyn
Seaway Lane
Seaway Ct.
Rec. Grnd.
The King's Gardens
Spa
Manscombe Plantation
Paignton Road
Stoneleigh Dr.
Broadstone
Broadley
Brendons
Winsford Rd.
Mendip Rd.
Quantocks Rd.
Cotswold Cl.
Lady Pk. Rd.
Pk. Cl.
Hawthorn
Manscombe Cl.
Chiltern Cl.
Drive
Broadpark
Road
Hollicombe Lake
Beavers Brook Cl.
Ten Acre Brake
Pentridge Av.
Manscombe
Barnfield
Broadpark
Old Mill Rd.
Underhill Rd.
Torbay Rd.
The King's Dr.
Livermead Sands
Livermead Hill
Avenue

20
A
B
C
D
1
2
3
4
5
6
17
19
TORQUAY
TQ2
TQ1
Hele
Hele Cross
Cemetery
Windmill Hill
Playing Field
Daison Wood
Quarries (dis.)
Torquay Comm. Coll.
Playing Fields
Bus Depot
Upton
Coach Sta.
Prim. Sch.
Stantaway Hill
Hosp.
South Devon College
Torre
St. Marychurch
Babbacombe Model Village
Cary Castle
Westlands Lower Sch.
Tessier Gds.
Cary Park
Plainmoor
Torquay Utd. F.C.
Ellacombe
Warberry Prim. Sc
Resr. (Cvd.)
Stentiford Hill
Pav.
Tennis Courts
English Riviera Centre
Swimming Pool
Torre Abbey
Spanish Barn
Abbey Park
Torre Abbey Meadows
Torre Abbey Sands
The King's Gardens
Rec. Grnd.
Two Parks
Torquay
Harbreck Rock
Corbyn's Beach
Corbyn's Head
Livermead Sands
Princess Pier
Landing Stage
Theatre
The Pavilion
Old Harbour
South Pier
Slipway
Beacon Quay
Aqualand
Beacon Cove
Haldon Pier
The Millstones
Prince of Wales Steps
Peaked Tor Cove
Braddons Cliffe
Winter Garden
Fleet Wlk. Shop Cen.
Union Sq. Shop. Cen.
Mkt
Court
Lib.
T.Hall
Museum
Bowl. Cen.
Offices
Shirley Towers
Passenger Ferry to Brixham May to September
TORBAY ROAD
A3022
A379
A379
STRAND
TEIGNMOUTH ROAD
HELE RD.
NEWTON ROAD
AVENUE ROAD
BARTON ROAD
CRICKETFIELD ROAD
WESTHILL ROAD
UPTON ROAD
ST. MARYCHURCH ROAD
BABBACOMBE ROAD
WINDSOR ROAD
ELLACOMBE CHURCH ROAD
PRINCES ROAD
LOWER WARBERRY ROAD
MIDDLE WARBERRY ROAD
HIGHER WARBERRY ROAD
ROCK ROAD
WARREN ROAD
ABBEY ROAD
UNION STREET
FLEET ST. (BUSES ONLY)
MEADFOOT ROAD
TORWOOD STREET
PARKHILL ROAD
BEACON HILL
FALKLAND RD.
THE KING'S DR.
RATHMORE RD.
CHESTNUT AV.
SHEDDEN HILL
CHURCH ST.
ST. MARYCHURCH
TRUMLANDS
91
92
65
64
63
66
515

21
E
F
G
H
93
294
66
65
64
63
1
2
3
4
5
6
ENGLISH CHANNEL
Oddicombe Beach
Blackball Rocks
Half Tide Rock
Babbacombe Beach
Breakwater
Withy Point
Theatre
The Downs
Quarry (dis.)
Gasking's Rock
Shelter Cove
Flagstaff Point
The Grove
Babbacombe
Babbacombe Pottery
Play. Fields
Quarry (Dis.)
Walls Hill
Works
Quarry (disused)
LONG QUARRY POINT
Community Centre
Walls Hill
Tennis Courts
Redgate Beach
Devil's Point
Anstey's Cove
Asheldon Copse
Burial Ground
Playing Field
Stoodley Knowle Convent Sch.
Tennis Courts
Playing Field
BLACK HEAD
Kent's Cavern
Wellswood
Brandy Cove
Hope Cove
Play. Field
Lincombe Slopes
Oxlea Copse
HOPE'S NOSE
Thatcher House
Manor Gardens
Manor House
Slipway
Meadfoot Beach
Thatcher Point
Thatcher Rock
Daddyhole Plain
A379
BABBACOMBE ROAD
WALLS HILL RD.
BEACH ROAD
DOWNS ROAD
ANSTEY'S COVE ROAD
BISHOP'S WALK
ILSHAM ROAD
ILSHAM CL.
ILSHAM CR.
ILSHAM MARINE DRIVE
MEADFOOT CL.
RICHMOND CL.
BISHOPS CLOSE
BISHOPS RISE
AVENUE DRIVE
WHIDBORNE AVENUE
WHIDBORNE CL.
THATCHER AVENUE
THATCHER AV.
THATCHER HEIGHTS
KILMORIE
KILMORIE CL.
LINCOMBE DRIVE
LINCOMBE HILL RD.
OXLEA ROAD
OXLEA CL.
THE WOODS
MIDDLE LINCOMBE ROAD
HIGHER LINCOMBE ROAD
RIDGEWAY ROAD
HALDON ROAD
HIGHER WOODFIELD ROAD
LOWER ERITH ROAD
ERITH ROAD
MEADFOOT SEA ROAD
HESKETH RD.
HESKETH CR.
ROYAL PINES
ST. MARK'S RD.
WARBERRY ROAD
LYDWELL ROAD
KENSEY CL.
DEN BROOKE CL.
HOLLYWATER CL.
PARK RD.
ASHELDON RD.
COLWYN CT.
WELLSWOOD AV.
WELLSWOOD PK.
WOODEND RD.
KENT'S LA.
KENT'S ROAD
ASHTON TER.
ST. MATTHIAS CH. RD.
ELLESMERE RD.
WELLSWOOD GS.
MARLBOROUGH AV.
GLENTHORNE CL.
DAPHNE CL.
LANGSTONE CL.
CHARMOUTH CL.
LOCKS HILL
SEATON CL.
BUDLEIGH CL.
REDGATE CL.
BRANSCOMBE CL.
ACRE LA.
GEORGIAN CT.
WARWICK CL.
FERNIVILLE
MANOR GS.
LYNCOMBE CRES.
BLENHEIM CL.
HALDON CL.
GAINSBOROUGH CL.
DANBY CL.
RIDGEWAY HEIGHTS

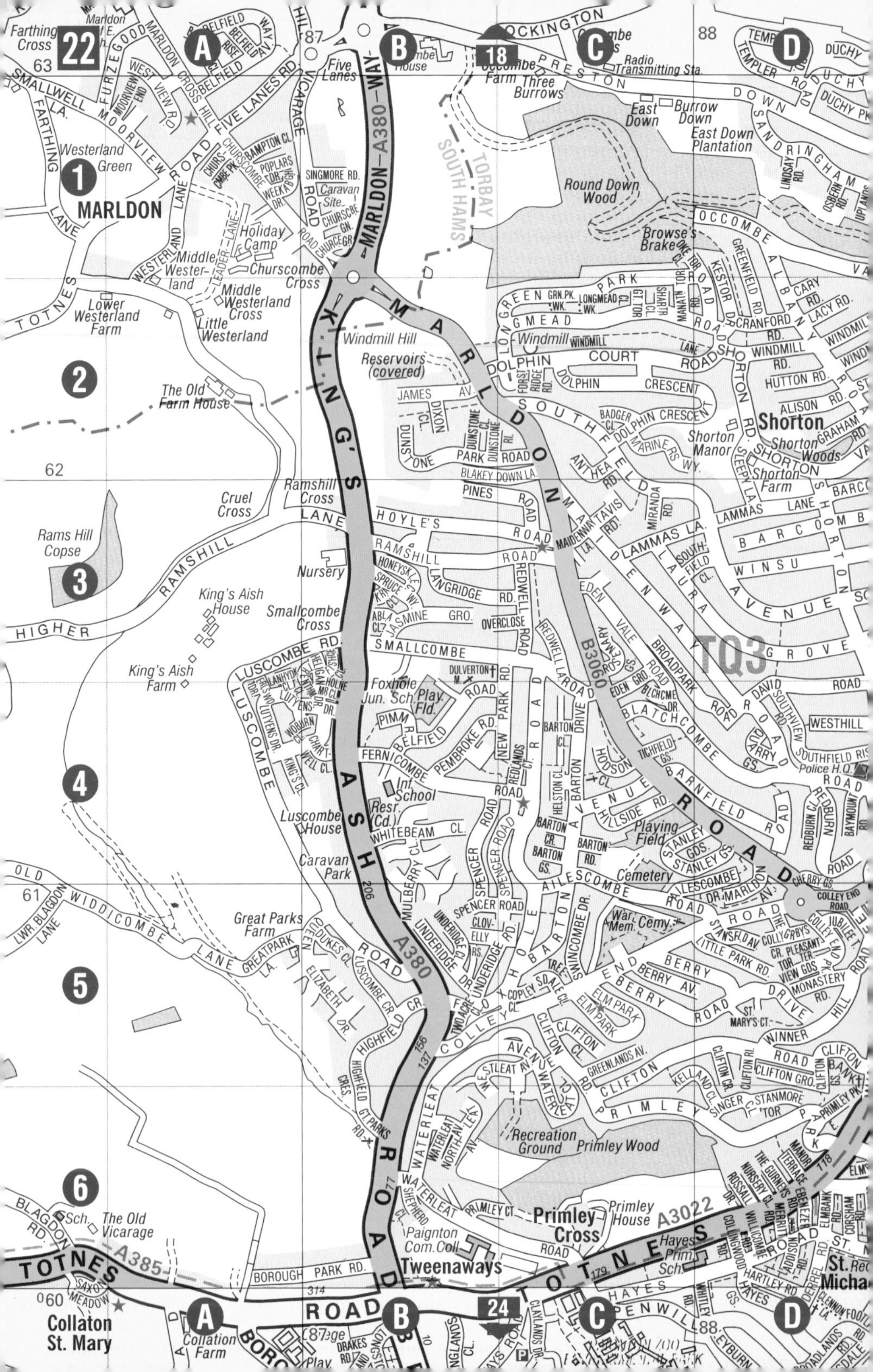

22
A
B
C
D
18
24
1
2
3
4
5
6
63
62
61
60
87
88
MARLDON
Farthing Cross
Westerland Green
Five Lanes
Five Lanes Rd.
Smallwell La.
Farthing Lane
Moorview Road
Furzegood
Marldon Cross Hill
Belfield Way
Vicarage Road
Singmore Rd.
Caravan Site
Holiday Camp
Middle Westerland
Churscombe Cross
Middle Westerland Cross
Little Westerland
Lower Westerland Farm
Westerland Lane
Totnes
Marldon–A380–Way
Kings Ash Road
Marldon Road
Windmill Hill
Reservoirs (covered)
The Old Farm House
Torbay
South Hams
Cockington
Preston
Occombe Farm
Three Burrows
Radio Transmitting Sta.
East Down
Burrow Down
East Down Plantation
Round Down Wood
Browse's Brake
Occombe Valley
Templer Road
Duchy
Sandringham
Longmead
Windmill
Dolphin Court
Dolphin Crescent
Southfield
Shorton
Shorton Manor
Shorton Woods
Shorton Farm
Shorton Road
Lammas Lane
Barcombe
Winsu
Laura Avenue
TQ3
Grove
Maidenway Road
Eden Vale Road
Broadpark Road
Blatchcombe
Barnfield Road
B3060
Ramshill Cross
Ramshill Lane
Hoyle's Road
Ramshill Road
Cruel Cross
Rams Hill Copse
Higher Ramshill
Nursery
King's Aish House
King's Aish Farm
Smallcombe Cross
Smallcombe
Langridge Rd.
Jasmine Gro.
Overclose
Redwell Road
Luscombe Rd.
Luscombe
Foxhole Jun. Sch.
Play. Fld.
Fernicombe
Belfield Road
Pembroke Rd.
New Park Rd.
Inf. School
Resr. (Cd.)
Luscombe House
Whitebeam Cl.
Caravan Park
Barton Avenue
Hillside Rd.
Playing Field
Cemetery
War Mem.
Cemy.
Ailescombe Road
Colley End Road
Old Widdicombe Lane
Lwr. Blagdon Lane
Great Parks Farm
Greatpark La.
Queen Elizabeth Dr.
Luscombe Cr.
Highfield Cres.
Underidge Dr.
Spencer Road
A380
Colley
Clifton Avenue
Berry Avenue
Monastery Road
Winner Hill
Clifton Road
Primley Park
Waterleat Road
Recreation Ground
Primley Wood
Primley Cross
Primley House
A3022
Totnes Road
Paignton Com. Coll.
Tweenaways
Borough Park Rd.
Hayes Prim. Sch.
Hayes Road
Penwill
St. Michael
Blagdon Rd.
Sch.
The Old Vicarage
A385
Saxon Meadow
Collaton St. Mary
Collaton Farm
Borough Road

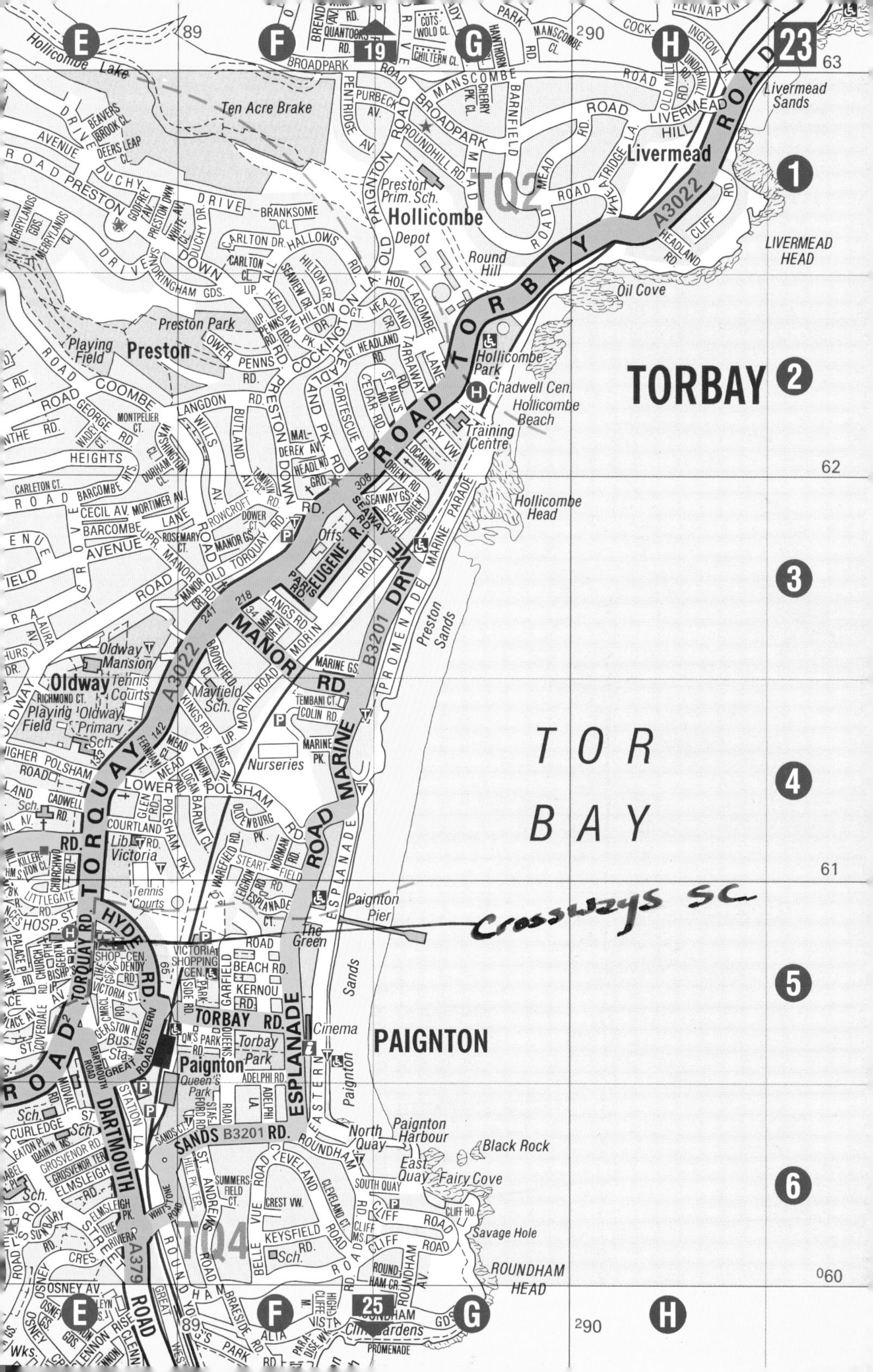

23
E
F
G
H
19
25
89
290
63
62
61
060
1
2
3
4
5
6
TQ2
TQ4
Hollicombe Lake
Ten Acre Brake
Livermead Sands
Livermead
LIVERMEAD HEAD
Livermead Hill
Cockington Lane
Broadpark Road
Manscombe Road
Barnfield Road
Wheatridge La.
Headland Rd.
Cliff Rd.
Preston Prim. Sch.
Hollicombe
Depot
Round Hill
Oil Cove
Hollicombe Park
Chadwell Cen.
Hollicombe Beach
Training Centre
Hollicombe Head
TORBAY
TOR BAY
Preston Park
Preston
Playing Field
Preston Down Rd.
Old Paignton Road
Cockington La.
Coombe Road
Barcombe Road
Grove Avenue
Manor Road
Old Torquay Rd.
Eugene Rd.
Seaway Rd.
Marine Drive
Marine Parade
Promenade
Preston Sands
A3022
B3201
Torquay Road
Oldway Mansion
Oldway
Tennis Courts
Playing Field
Oldway Primary Sch.
Mayfield Sch.
Morin Road
Marine Gs.
Nurseries
Higher Polsham Road
Lower Polsham Rd.
Victoria
Lib.
Hyde Rd.
Esplanade Road
Paignton Pier
Crossways SC
The Green
Victoria Shopping Cen.
Shop. Cen.
Beach Rd.
Kernou Rd.
Torbay Rd.
Torbay Park
Paignton
Queen's Park
Bus. Sta.
Great Western Road
Station La.
Cinema
Paignton Sands
PAIGNTON
Eastern Esplanade
North Quay
Paignton Harbour
Black Rock
East Quay
Fairy Cove
South Quay
Sands Rd.
Roundham Rd.
Cleveland Road
Belle Vue Road
Keysfield Rd.
Cliff Road
Cliff Ho.
Savage Hole
ROUNDHAM HEAD
Dartmouth Road
A379
Roundham Av.
Cliff Gardens
Promenade

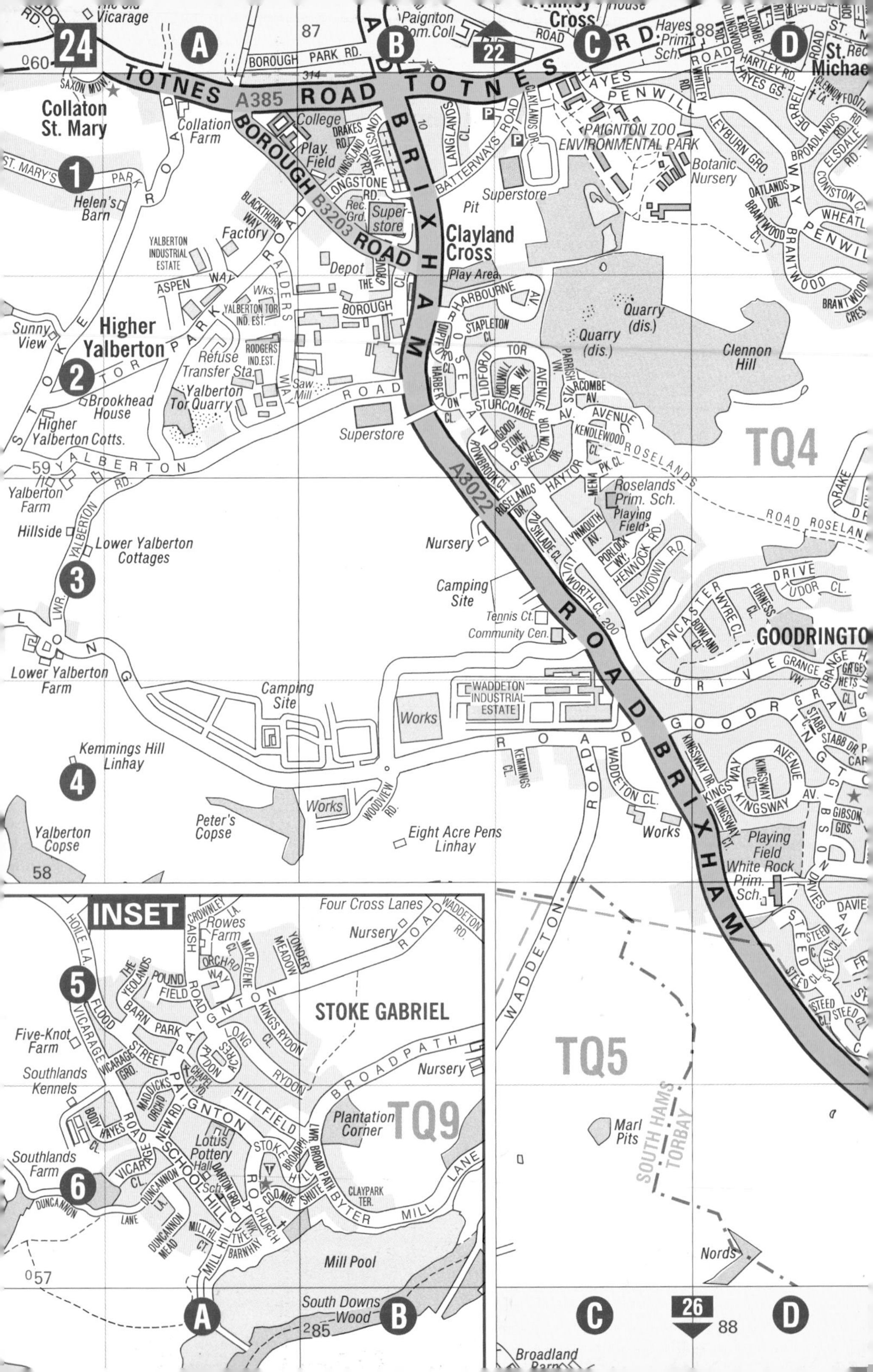
24
22
26
A
B
C
D
1
2
3
4
5
6
TOTNES ROAD
A385
BOROUGH ROAD
B3203
BRIXHAM ROAD
A3022
Collaton St. Mary
Higher Yalberton
Clayland Cross
Paignton Zoo Environmental Park
Clennon Hill
Goodrington
TQ4
TQ5
TQ9
INSET
STOKE GABRIEL
Yalberton Industrial Estate
Waddeton Industrial Estate
Superstore
Quarry (dis.)
Roselands Prim. Sch.
White Rock Prim. Sch.
Lower Yalberton Farm
Yalberton Copse
Peter's Copse
Kemmings Hill Linhay
Eight Acre Pens Linhay
Marl Pits
Mill Pool
South Downs Wood
Plantation Corner
Lotus Pottery
Southlands Farm
Five-Knot Farm
Four Cross Lanes
SOUTH HAMS
TORBAY
Nords
Broadland Barn

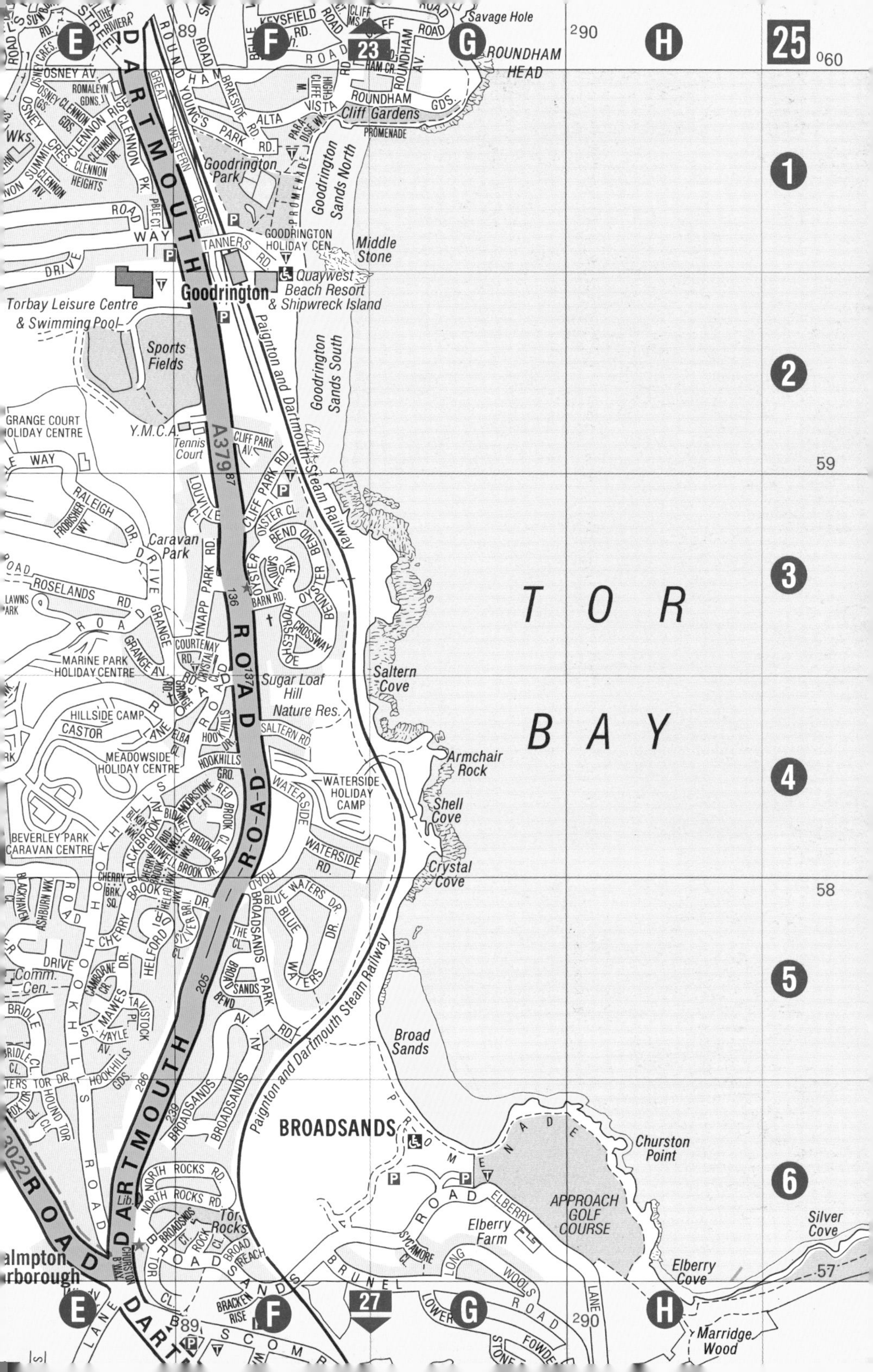

Savage Hole
ROUNDHAM HEAD
23
Cliff Gardens
PROMENADE
Goodrington Park
Goodrington Sands North
Middle Stone
GOODRINGTON HOLIDAY CEN.
Goodrington
Quaywest Beach Resort & Shipwreck Island
Torbay Leisure Centre & Swimming Pool
Sports Fields
Goodrington Sands South
Paignton and Dartmouth Steam Railway
GRANGE COURT HOLIDAY CENTRE
Y.M.C.A.
Tennis Court
A379
Caravan Park
DARTMOUTH ROAD
T O R
B A Y
MARINE PARK HOLIDAY CENTRE
Sugar Loaf Hill Nature Res.
Saltern Cove
HILLSIDE CAMP
MEADOWSIDE HOLIDAY CENTRE
WATERSIDE HOLIDAY CAMP
Armchair Rock
Shell Cove
BEVERLEY PARK CARAVAN CENTRE
Crystal Cove
Comm. Cen.
Broad Sands
BROADSANDS
Churston Point
APPROACH GOLF COURSE
Elberry Farm
Silver Cove
Elberry Cove
Tor Rocks
Lib.
27
Marridge Wood
B3022
E F G H
1 2 3 4 5 6
290 060 59 58 57

Water Lane Plantation
Waddeton Pool
Pool Plantation
WADDETON ROAD
Waddeton Barton
WADDETON RD.
WADDETON COTTS.
WADDETON
STOKE ROAD
East Farm
Waddeton Home farm
Manor Ho. (rems.of)
Waddeton Court
Broadland Barn
Quarry (dis.)
Kiln Copse
Galmpton Strip
Nords
24
TQ9
Sandridge Bottom
Kennel Wood
Toms Plantation
Tors Wood
Barn Wood
GABRIEL
PORT HILL
Sewage Works
East Wood
The Cliffs
Slate Wood
Sandridge Boat House
Slipways
Roundabout
Black Earth Wood
Grotto Wood
Waddeton Quarry (dis.)
Galmpton Quarry (dis.)
Boat House
Quay
The Banks
Galmpton Kilns
Quays
Dartside Boat Park
RIVER
Higher Gurrow Point
Galmpton Creek
Yacht Yard
KILN
Mill Point
MILL LANE
Gurrow Point House
Lower Gurrow Point
Flat Owers
Old Mill Farm
HOOK LANE
Brim Hill
Brimhill Plantation
Reservoir (covered)
Lower Greenway
Hook Bottom
Hare Wood
RIVERSIDE RD.
HAM LA.
DITTISHAM
GREENWAY ROAD
Down Copse
Hunterswood
Lodge
THE LANE
THE QUAY
Pier
Pontoon
Greenway Quay
Meadow Cottages
THE LEVEL
MANOR ST.
Ferry (foot)
Ferry Cottage
Greenway House
Greenway Tunnel
TQ6
Slipway
South Lodge
Higher Greenway
Lower Dittisham
The Old Rectory
Binhay Copse
Maypool (Youth Hostel)
Tippity Van
Anchor Stone
Oakham Hill
The River Farm
River Farm Cottage
River Farm House
Vipers Quay
DART
Maypool Cottage
Greenway Viaduct
Reservoir (covered)
Pond
Boat House
Glebe Plantation
Hamblyn's Coombe
Parson's Mud
Waterfields Cottage
LORD'S WOOD
Paignton and Dartmouth Steam Railway
A
B
C
D
1
2
3
4
5
6
57
56
55
54
87
88

27
25
28
E
F
G
H
1
2
3
4
5
6
TQ4
TQ5
Windy Corner
DARTMOUTH ROAD
A3022
BRIXHAM ROAD
KENNELS ROAD
A379
BASCOMBE
BRUNEL ROAD
ELBERRY LANE
Elberry Farm
Elberry Cove
Marridge Wood
CHURSTON GOLF COURSE
CHURSTON FERRERS
Churston
Churston Court Farm
Churston Court
Greenmarch
Windmill (disused)
Recreation Ground
Club Ho.
Churston Grammar Sch.
Tennis Court
Playing Fields
Paignton and Dartmouth Steam Railway
Brokenbury Quarry (dis.)
Kart Track
Park & Ride
Churston Cross
Alston
Lodge
Alston Farm
Nurseries
Higher Alston
Reservoir (covered)
Alston Reservoir (covered)
Garden Plantation
Barn Copse
Gramercy Hall School
LUPTON PARK
The Down
Windmill Copse
Coronation Plantation
West Ground
Lupton Barton Farm
Big Wood
Guzzle Down
Kennel Wood West
Kennel Wood East
Kennels
Kennel Wood
Southbank
Hillhead Reservoir
SOUTH HAMS
TORBAY
COMBE LANE
ALSTON LANE
KINGSWEAR RD.
GREENWAY ROAD
COPYTHORNE RD.

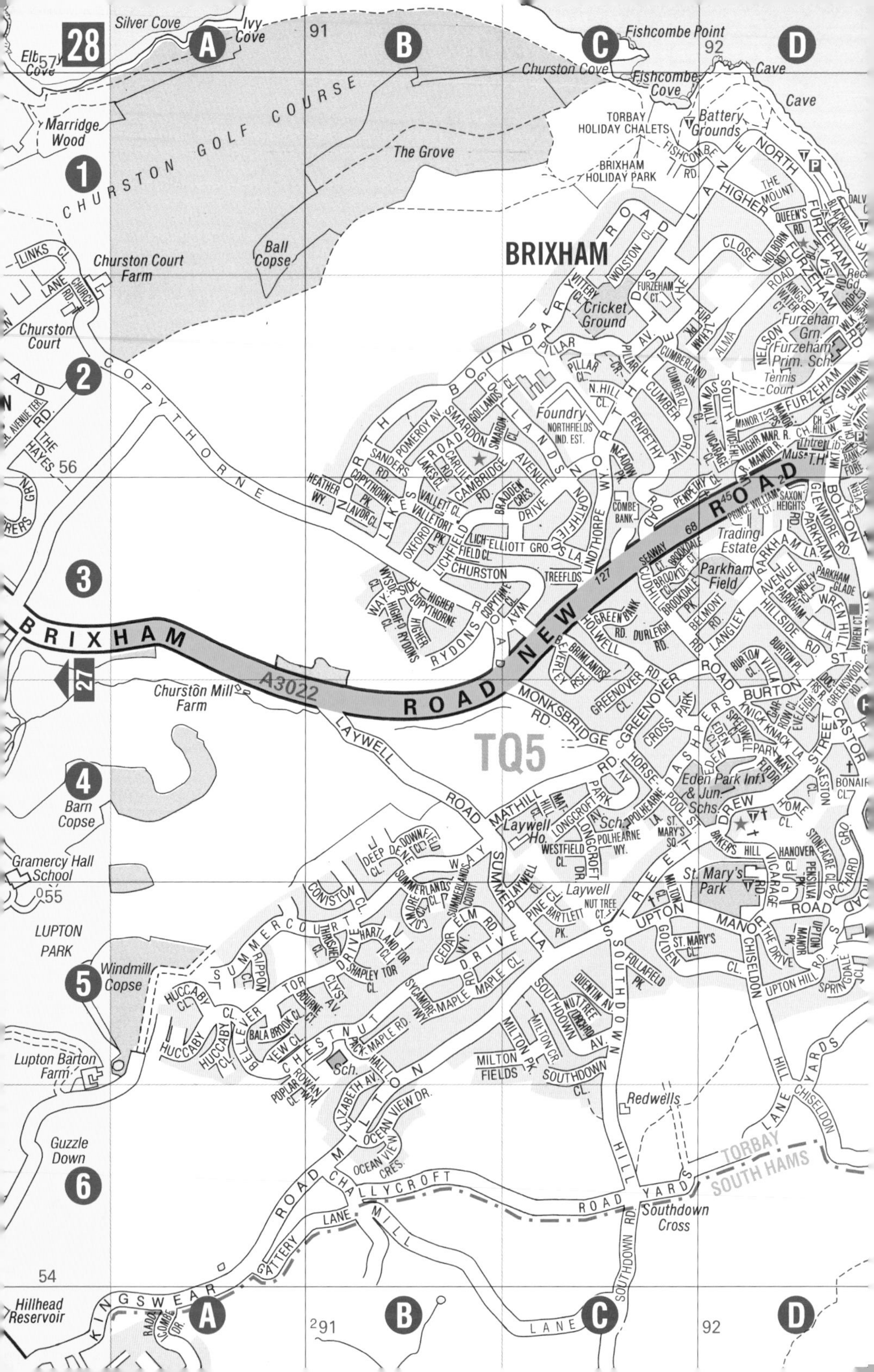
Silver Cove
Ivy Cove
91
Fishcombe Point
92
Churston Cove
Fishcombe Cove
Cave
Cave
Marridge Wood
CHURSTON GOLF COURSE
The Grove
TORBAY HOLIDAY CHALETS
Battery Grounds
BRIXHAM HOLIDAY PARK
Ball Copse
LINKS CL.
Churston Court Farm
BRIXHAM
Churston Court
Cricket Ground
Furzeham Grn.
Furzeham Prim. Sch.
Tennis Court
COPYTHORNE
Foundry
NORTHFIELDS IND. EST.
56
HIGHER LANE
NORTH FURZEHAM RD.
BOUNDARY ROAD
NORTHFIELDS LA.
PENPETHY RD.
NEW ROAD
Trading Estate
Parkham Field
BRIXHAM ROAD
A3022
27
Churston Mill Farm
ROAD NEW
LAYWELL ROAD
MONKSBRIDGE RD.
TQ5
Barn Copse
Gramercy Hall School
Laywell Ho.
Eden Park Inf. & Jun. Schs.
St. Mary's Park
Laywell
55
LUPTON PARK
Windmill Copse
SUMMERCOURT
CHESTNUT DRIVE
UPTON MANOR ROAD
Lupton Barton Farm
Sch.
MILTON FIELDS
Redwells
Guzzle Down
MILTON ROAD
CHALLYCROFT ROAD
YARDS
Southdown Cross
TORBAY
SOUTH HAMS
MILL LANE
GATTERY LANE
54
Hillhead Reservoir
KINGSWEAR
291
92
LANE

E
93
F
G
294
H
57
Passenger Ferry to Torquay May to September
THE BREAKWATER
HARBOUR
Brixham Marina
Shoalstone Beach
Shoalstone Point
Bathing Pool
Coastguard Station
Breakwater Beach
Jetty
The Hard
Slipway
Quay
Berry Head Quarry (dis.)
Lighthouse
Ash Hole Cavern
Berry Head Farm
BERRY HEAD ROAD
VICTORIA RD.
BERRY CT.
WOLBOROUGH GDNS.
LANDS RD.
HEATH CT.
HEATH RISE
HEATH ROAD
Orphanage
New Pier
HARBOUR
Beacon
BERRY HEAD COUNTRY PARK
Old Redoubt
Berry Head Fort
BERRY HEAD
TORBAY CT.
MARINA DRIVE
PARK CT.
ACOTT GDS.
WASHBOURNE CL.
MARINA CL.
WALL PARK HOLIDAY CENTRE
KING ST.
NEW QUAY LA.
MOORINGS REACH
Golden Hind
HEATH PK.
RIDGEMARK CL.
ANCHORAGE CL.
CLOSE
PARK ROAD
NORTH VIEW RD.
GARLIC REA
GARLIC REA
RANSCOMBE CL.
WALL PARK CL.
HAYCOCK LA.
The Bungalow
Beacon
Old Redoubt
Visitors Centre
ELKINS HILL
GREAT REA
LOWER REA RD.
WALL RD.
LOUVILLE CAMP
Football Ground
ROAD
56
BROAD REA
REA RD.
MOUNT RD.
LYTE'S RD.
WESTOVER CL.
ROAD
CENTRY RD.
CENTRY CT.
Mew Stone
Cod Rock
Brixham Leis. Cen.
WINDMILL CLOSE
Brixham Comm. Coll.
Brixham C. of E. Inf. Sch.
Play. Fld.
RANSCOMBE
Playing Field
LANDSCOVE HOLIDAY VILLAGE
GILLARD
Shoalstone Swim. Pool
POUNDSGATE CL.
HILL PK. CL.
HILL PK. RD.
MARINA RD.
Durl Head
Durl Rock
REA BARN CL.
HIGHER
Astley Park
NEW PK. CL.
ROAD
BARN
SEA LANE
DOUGLAS AV.
LANE
CRES.
SELLICK AV.
QUEEN'S
EDINBURGH RD.
PEASEDITCH
Playing Field
MEADOWS
ROAD
WISHINGS ROAD
MUDSTONE
LANE
HIGHER PENN
ST. MARY'S BAY
ST. MARY'S BAY HOLIDAY CEN.
DOLPHIN HOLIDAY CEN.
HIGHER BRIXHAM
Mussel Rock
055
ROAD
SHARKHAM POINT CARAVAN PARK
Mine (disused)
SOUTH BAY HOLIDAY CAMP
Shaft (dis.)
Sharkham Point
Mag Rock
ENGLISH CHANNEL
Cliff
54
1
2
3
4
5
6
E
93
F
G
94
H

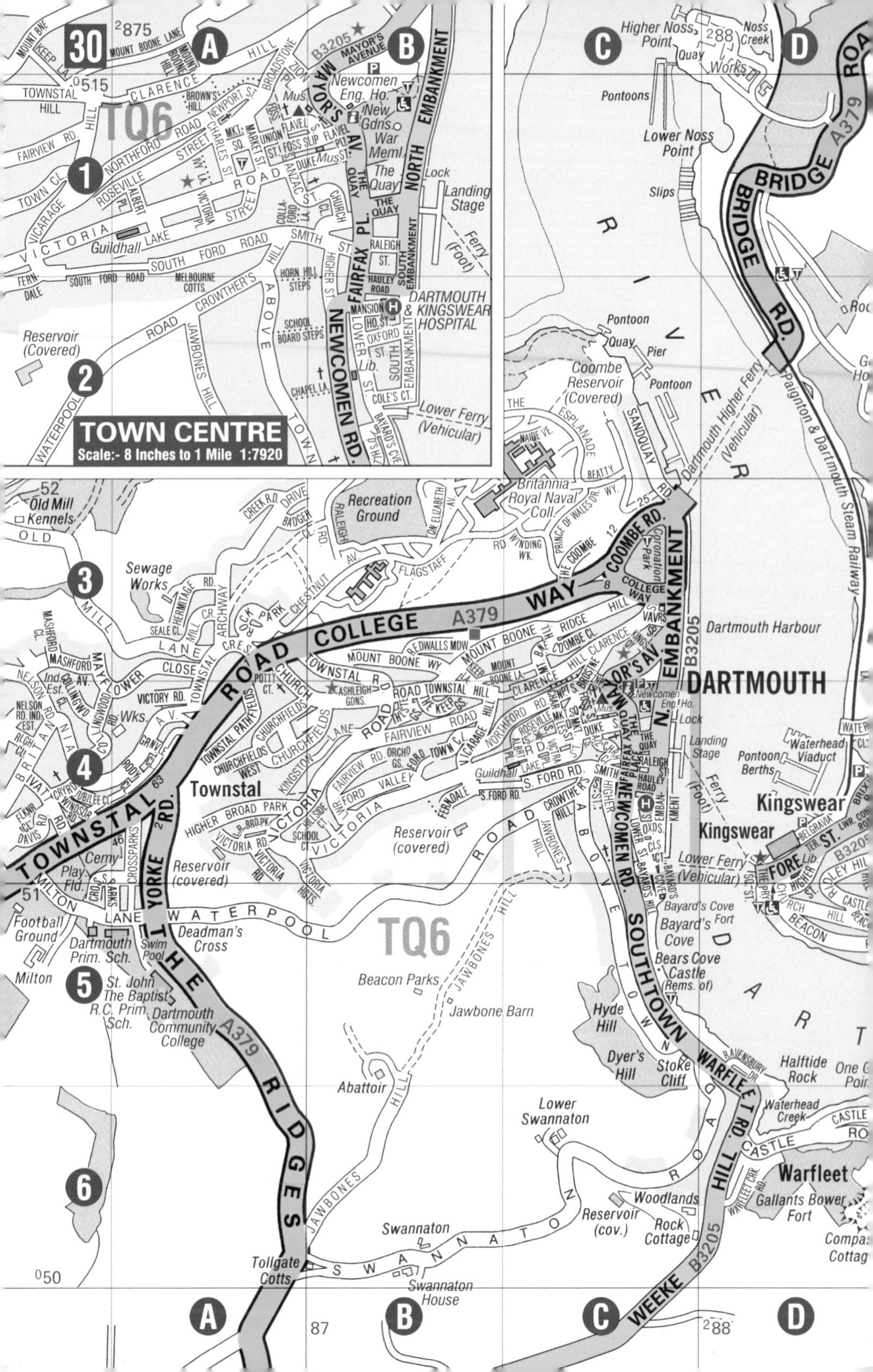
TOWN CENTRE
Scale:- 8 Inches to 1 Mile 1:7920
DARTMOUTH
Kingswear
Townstal
TQ6
Britannia Royal Naval Coll.
Dartmouth Harbour
Dartmouth Higher Ferry (Vehicular)
Lower Ferry (Vehicular)
Ferry (Foot)
Paignton & Dartmouth Steam Railway
DARTMOUTH KINGSWEAR HOSPITAL
Guildhall
Newcomen Eng. Ho.
New Gdns.
War Meml.
Landing Stage
Lock
Higher Noss Point
Lower Noss Point
Noss Creek
Quay Works
Pontoons
Slips
Pontoon
Quay
Pier
Coombe Reservoir (Covered)
Reservoir (Covered)
Reservoir (covered)
Reservoir (cov.)
Recreation Ground
Sewage Works
Old Mill Kennels
Ind. Est.
Wks.
Cemy.
Play. Fld.
Football Ground
Milton
Dartmouth Prim. Sch.
Swim Pool
St. John The Baptist R.C. Prim. Sch.
Dartmouth Community College
Deadman's Cross
Beacon Parks
Jawbone Barn
Abattoir
Hyde Hill
Dyer's Hill
Stoke Cliff
Bayard's Cove
Bayard's Cove Fort
Bears Cove Castle (Rems. of)
Lower Swannaton
Swannaton
Swannaton House
Woodlands
Rock Cottage
Tollgate Cotts.
Waterhead Viaduct
Pontoon Berths
Halftide Rock
Waterhead Creek
Warfleet
Gallants Bower Fort
COLLEGE WAY
A379
B3205
COLLEGE ROAD
TOWNSTAL ROAD
THE RIDGES
YORKE RD.
NORTH EMBANKMENT
SOUTH EMBANKMENT
NEWCOMEN RD.
SOUTHTOWN
WARFLEET RD.
WEEKE HILL
BRIDGE RD.
MAYOR'S AV.
FAIRFAX PL.
VICTORIA ROAD
SOUTH FORD ROAD
CROWTHER'S HILL
JAWBONES HILL
WATERPOOL ROAD
SWANNATON ROAD
MILTON LANE
MOUNT BOONE
CLARENCE HILL
NORTHFORD ROAD
FAIRVIEW RD.
TOWNSTAL HILL
CHURCHFIELDS
MAYFLOWER CLOSE
OLD MILL LANE
FORE ST.
CASTLE ROAD
A B C D
1 2 3 4 5 6
87
288
050
2875
0515
52
51
46
63

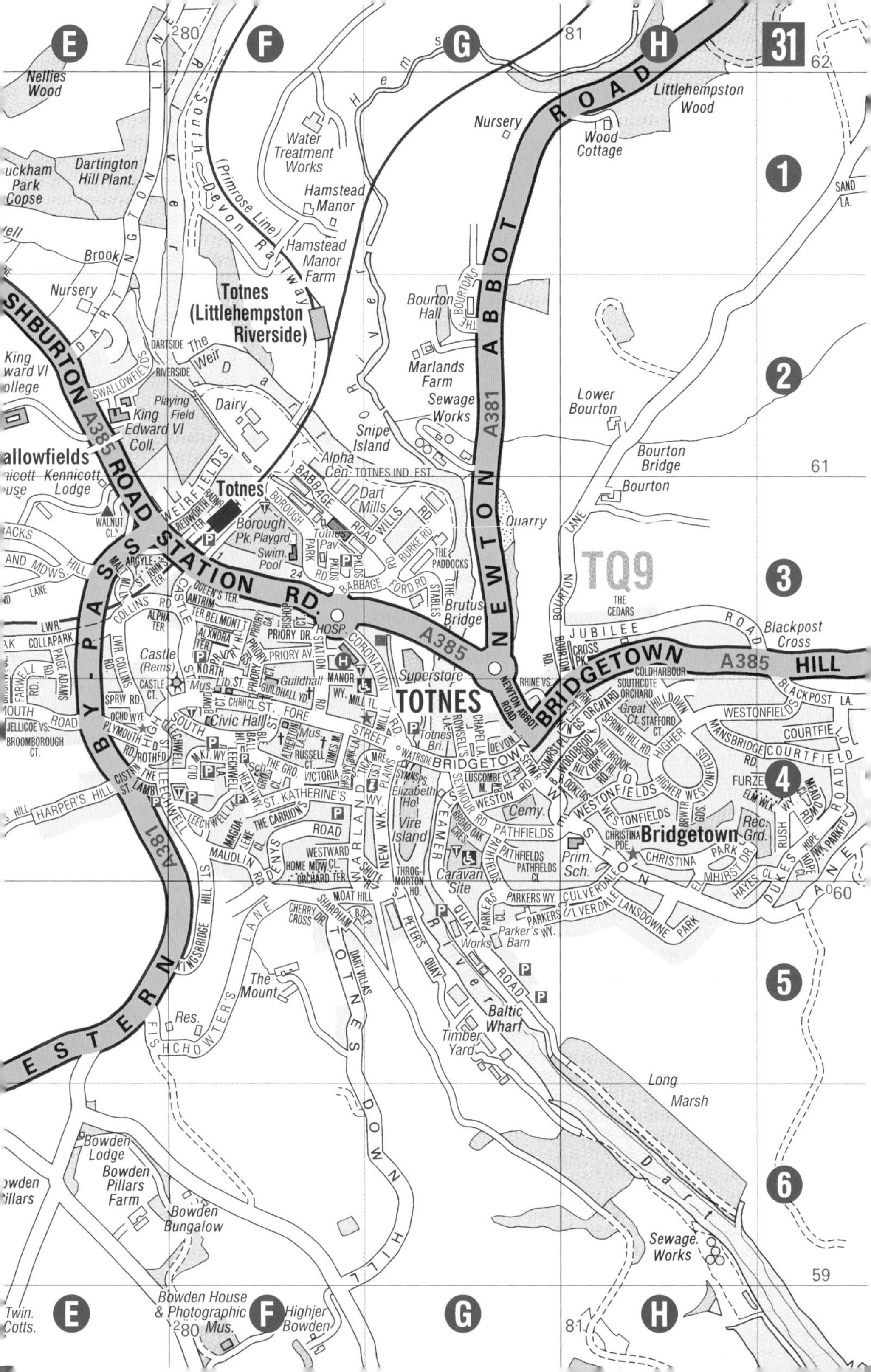

E
F
G
H
1
2
3
4
5
6
280
81
62
61
60
59
Nellies Wood
Dartington Hill Plant.
Water Treatment Works
Hamstead Manor
Hamstead Manor Farm
Nursery
Littlehempston Wood
Wood Cottage
NEWTON ABBOT ROAD
A381
South Devon Railway
(Primrose Line)
River Dart
Totnes (Littlehempston Riverside)
Bourton Hall
Marlands Farm
Sewage Works
Snipe Island
Lower Bourton
Bourton Bridge
Bourton
Bourton Lane
King Edward VI Coll.
Playing Field
Dairy
The Weir
Kennicott Lodge
Totnes
Borough Pk.
Playgrd.
Swim. Pool
Alpha Cen.
TOTNES IND. EST.
Dart Mills
BABBAGE ROAD
STATION RD.
A385
BY-PASS
ASHBURTON ROAD
Quarry
TQ9
THE CEDARS
JUBILEE ROAD
Blackpost Cross
BRIDGETOWN HILL
Brutus Bridge
HOSP.
Castle (Rems)
Mus.
Guildhall
Civic Hall
TOTNES
Superstore
FORE STREET
Totnes Bri.
BRIDGETOWN
Vire Island
Elizabeth Ho.
Cemy.
Bridgetown
Prim. Sch.
Rec. Grd.
Caravan Site
Parker's Barn
Baltic Wharf
Timber Yard
Long Marsh
Sewage Works
WESTERN BY-PASS
A381
The Mount
Res.
FISHCHOWTER'S LANE
TOTNES DOWN HILL
KINGSBRIDGE HILL
Bowden Lodge
Bowden Pillars Farm
Bowden Bungalow
Bowden House & Photographic Mus.
Highjer Bowden
Twin. Cotts.

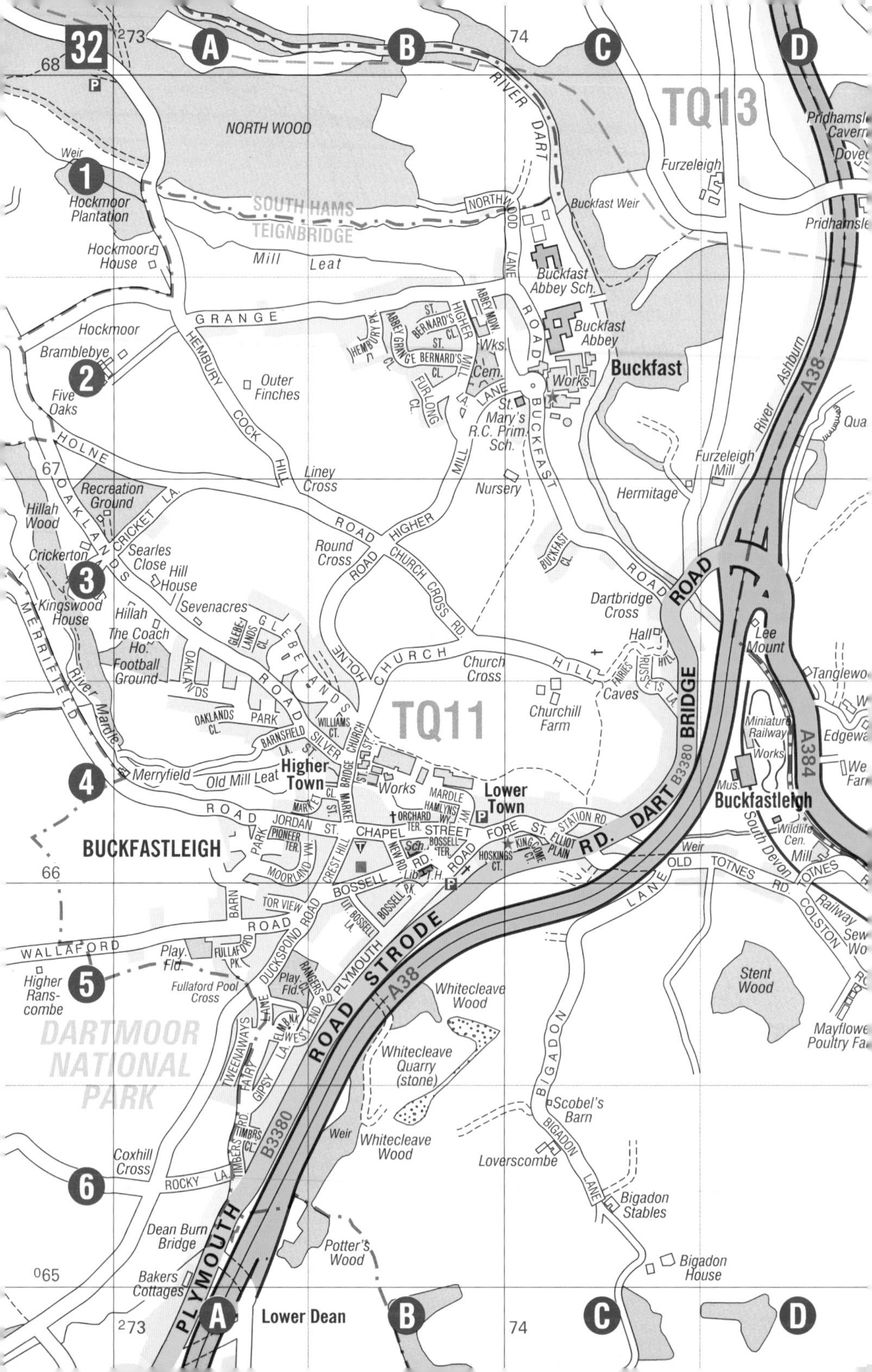
A
B
C
D
1
2
3
4
5
6
273
74
68
67
66
065
TQ13
TQ11
NORTH WOOD
RIVER DART
SOUTH HAMS
TEIGNBRIDGE
Mill Leat
Weir
Hockmoor Plantation
Hockmoor House
Hockmoor
Bramblebye
Five Oaks
GRANGE
HEMBURY COCK HILL
Outer Finches
Liney Cross
HOLNE ROAD
Recreation Ground
Hillah Wood
Crickerton
Kingswood House
CRICKET LA.
Searles Close
Hill House
Sevenacres
Hillah
The Coach Ho.
Football Ground
OAKLANDS
MERRIFIELD
River Mardle
Merryfield
Old Mill Leat
Higher Town
Lower Town
BUCKFASTLEIGH
GLEBELANDS
OAKLANDS CL.
PARK
BARNSFIELD LA.
SILVER ST.
WILLIAMS CT.
CHURCH ST.
Works
MARDLE WY.
HAMLYNS WY.
ORCHARD TER.
MARKET ST.
JORDAN ST.
CHAPEL STREET
PIONEER TER.
MOORLAND VW.
CREST HILL
NEW RD.
Sch.
BOSSELL TER.
BOSSELL RD.
BOSSELL PK.
LIT. BOSSELL LA.
Lib.
T.H.
FORE ST.
HOSKINGS CT.
KINGCOME CT.
ELLIOT PLAIN
STATION RD.
TOR VIEW
BARN ROAD
DUCKSPOND ROAD
WALLAFORD
Play. Fld.
FULLAFORD PK.
Higher Ranscombe
Fullaford Pool Cross
RANGERS CL.
WEST END RD.
PLYMOUTH RD.
STRODE ROAD
A38
B3380
DARTMOOR NATIONAL PARK
TWEENAWAYS
FAIRY LA.
GIPSY LA.
TIMBERS RD.
TIMBERS CL.
Coxhill Cross
ROCKY LA.
Dean Burn Bridge
Bakers Cottages
Lower Dean
PLYMOUTH ROAD
Whitecleave Wood
Whitecleave Quarry (stone)
Potter's Wood
Round Cross
CHURCH CROSS RD.
HIGHER MILL LANE
Church Cross
CHURCH HILL
Churchill Farm
Caves
FAIRIES HILL
RUSSETS LA.
Hall
Dartbridge Cross
DART BRIDGE ROAD
Nursery
BUCKFAST ROAD
BUCKFAST CL.
St. Mary's R.C. Prim. Sch.
NORTHWOOD LANE
Buckfast Abbey Sch.
Buckfast Abbey
Buckfast
Buckfast Weir
Works
Wks.
Cem.
ABBEY MDW.
ST. BERNARD'S CL.
HEMBURY PK.
ABBEY GRANGE CL.
FURLONG CL.
Furzeleigh
Furzeleigh Mill
Hermitage
River Ashburn
Lee Mount
Miniature Railway
Buckfastleigh
Mus.
Wildlife Cen.
South Devon Railway
OLD TOTNES RD.
TOTNES LANE
COLSTON
Stent Wood
A384
BIGADON LANE
Scobel's Barn
Loverscombe
Bigadon Stables
Bigadon House

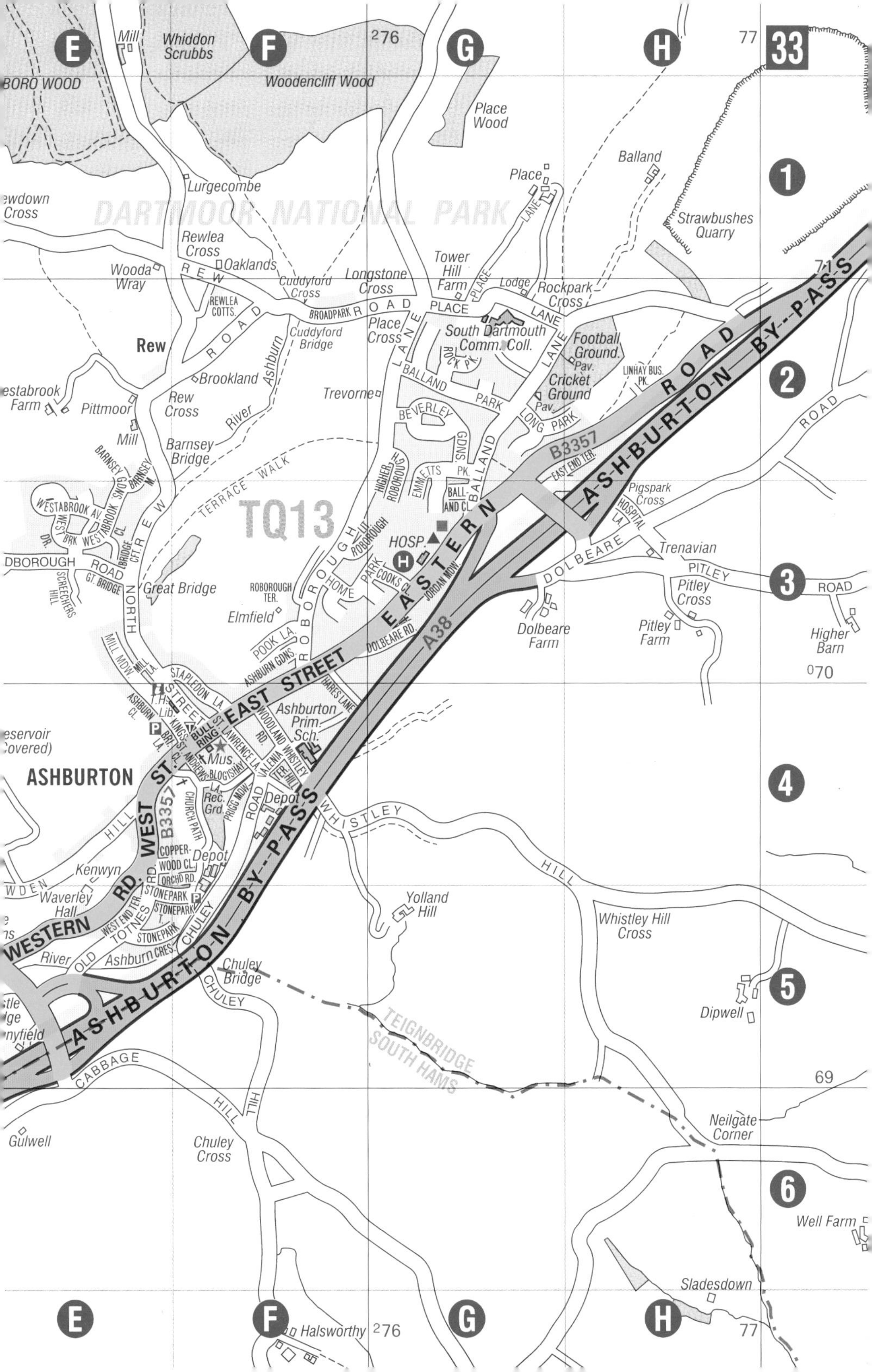

Whiddon Scrubbs
Woodencliff Wood
Place Wood
DARTMOOR NATIONAL PARK
Lurgecombe
Rewlea Cross
Oaklands
Wooda Wray
Cuddyford Cross
Longstone Cross
Tower Hill Farm
Rockpark Cross
Balland
Strawbushes Quarry
South Dartmouth Comm. Coll.
Football Ground
Cricket Ground
Rew
Brookland
Rew Cross
Cuddyford Bridge
Place Cross
Trevorne
Pittmoor
Mill
Barnsey Bridge
TQ13
Great Bridge
Elmfield
Dolbeare Farm
Pitley Cross
Pitley Farm
Trenavian
Pigspark Cross
Higher Barn
ASHBURTON
Ashburton Prim. Sch.
Mus.
Depot
Kenwyn
Waverley Hall
Yolland Hill
Whistley Hill Cross
Chuley Bridge
TEIGNBRIDGE
SOUTH HAMS
Dipwell
Neilgate Corner
Gulwell
Chuley Cross
Well Farm
Sladesdown
Halsworthy
EASTERN ROAD
ASHBURTON BY-PASS
EAST STREET
WEST ST.
WESTERN RD.
B3357
A38

INDEX

Including Streets, Industrial Estates, Selected Subsidiary Addresses and Selected Places of Interest.

HOW TO USE THIS INDEX

1. Each street name is followed by its Posttown or Postal Locality and then by its map reference; e.g. Abbotsbury Rd. *New A* —1G **11** is in the Newton Abbot Posttown and is to be found in square 1G on page **11**. The page number being shown in bold type.
   A strict alphabetical order is followed in which Av., Rd., St., etc. (though abbreviated) are read in full and as part of the street name; e.g. Ashridge Gdns. appears after Ash Pk. but before Ash Rd.

2. Streets and a selection of Subsidiary names not shown on the Maps, appear in the index in *Italics* with the thoroughfare to which it is connected shown in brackets; e.g. *Abbotswell Cotts. New A —6G **11** (off Ford Rd.)*

3. An example of a selected place of interest is **Aqualand. —6C 20**

4. Map references shown in brackets; e.g. Above Town. ***Dart*** —4C **30** (2A **30**) refer to entries that also appear on the large scale on page **30**.

GENERAL ABBREVIATIONS

All : Alley
App : Approach
Arc : Arcade
Av : Avenue
Bk : Back
Boulevd : Boulevard
Bri : Bridge
B'way : Broadway
Bldgs : Buildings
Bus : Business
Cvn : Caravan
Cen : Centre
Chu : Church
Chyd : Churchyard
Circ : Circle
Cir : Circus
Clo : Close
Comn : Common
Cotts : Cottages
Ct : Court
Cres : Crescent
Cft : Croft
Dri : Drive
E : East
Embkmt : Embankment
Est : Estate
Fld : Field
Gdns : Gardens
Gth : Garth
Ga : Gate
Gt : Great
Grn : Green
Gro : Grove
Ho : House
Ind : Industrial
Info : Information
Junct : Junction
La : Lane
Lit : Little
Lwr : Lower
Mc : Mac
Mnr : Manor
Mans : Mansions
Mkt : Market
Mdw : Meadow
M : Mews
Mt : Mount
Mus : Museum
N : North
Pal : Palace
Pde : Parade
Pk : Park
Pas : Passage
Pl : Place
Quad : Quadrant
Res : Residential
Ri : Rise
Rd : Road
Shop : Shopping
S : South
Sq : Square
Sta : Station
St : Street
Ter : Terrace
Trad : Trading
Up : Upper
Va : Vale
Vw : View
Vs : Villas
Vis : Visitors
Wlk : Walk
W : West
Yd : Yard

POSTTOWN AND POSTAL LOCALITY ABBREVIATIONS

Abbot : Abbotskerswell
Ashb : Ashburton
Ashtn : Ashprington
Bart : Barton
Bish : Bishopsteignton
Black : Blackawton
Blag : Blagdon
Bov T : Bovey Tracey
Brad V : Bradley Valley
Brix : Brixham
Broads : Broadsands
Buck : Buckfast
Buckf : Buckfastleigh
Chag : Chagford
Chel : Chelston
Chud : Chudleigh
Chur F : Churston Ferrers
Coff : Coffinswell
Combe : Combeinteignhead
Comp : Compton
Dac : Daccombe
Dart : Dartmouth
Daw : Dawlish
Daw W : Dawlish Warren
Dec I : Decoy Ind. Est.
Den : Denbury
Dit : Dittisham
Elcm : Ellacombe
Galm : Galmpton
Good : Goodrington
Hacc : Haccombe
Harb T : Harbour, The
Hbtn : Harberton
Heath : Heathfield
Hele : Hele
Holc : Holcombe
Ippn : Ipplepen
Kgstn : Kingsteignton
Kgswl : Kingskerswell
Kgswr : Kingswear
Lust : Lustleigh
Maid : Maidencombe
Marl : Marldon
Neth : Netherton
New A : Newton Abbot
Ogwl : Ogwell
Paign : Paignton
Pres : Preston
St M : St Marychurch
Sand : Sandygate
Shal : Shaldon
Sto F : Stoke Fleming
Sto G : Stoke Gabriel
Stone : Stoneycombe
Stov : Stover
Teign : Teignmouth
Tngrc : Teigngrace
Torq : Torquay
Tot : Totnes
Town I : Townstal Ind. Est.
Tuck : Tuckenhay
Wadd : Waddeton
Whil : Whilborough

INDEX

Abbey Clo. *Bov T* —3B **4**
Abbey Clo. *Teign* —2E **9**
Abbey Cres. *Torq* —5B **20**
Abbey Grange Clo. *Buck* —2B **32**
Abbey Mdw. *Buck* —2B **32**
Abbey Rd. *Torq* —4B **20**
Abbey Rd. *Bov T* —2B **4**
Abbotsbury Rd. *New A* —1G **11**
Abbotshill Cvn. Pk. *Abbot* —1B **14**
Abbotsridge Dri. *Ogwl* —4E **11**
*Abbotswell Cotts. New A —6G **11** (off Ford Rd.)*
Abbotswood. *Kgstn* —3G **7**
Abbrook Av. *Kgstn* —2E **7**
Abelia Clo. *Paign* —3B **22**
Above Town. *Dart* —4C **30** (2A **30**)
Acacia Clo. *Kgstn* —6F **7**
Acadia Rd. *Torq* —5F **21**
Acre La. *Torq* —3F **21**
Addison Rd. *New A* —3B **12**
Addison Rd. *Paign* —6D **22**
Adelphi La. *Paign* —6F **23**
Adelphi Rd. *Paign* —5F **23**
Admirals Wlk. *Teign* —1C **8**
Ailescombe Dri. *Paign* —5C **22**
Ailescombe Rd. *Paign* —5C **22**
Aish Rd. *Sto G* —5A **24**
Alandale Clo. *Teign* —3E **9**
Alandale Rd. *Teign* —3E **9**
Albany Rd. *Paign* —1D **22**
Albany St. *New A* —2H **11**
Alberta Ct. *Teign* —4E **9**
Albert Pl. *Dart* —1A **30**
Albert Rd. *Torq* —4C **20**
Albert St. *Daw* —4D **2**
Albert Ter. *New A* —2H **11**
Albert Ter. *Bov T* —3B **4**
Albion Hill. *New A* —3H **11**
Albion St. *Shal* —6C **8**
Alder Clo. *New A* —5C **12**
Alder Clo. *Teign* —3D **8**
Alders Way. *Paign* —1A **24**
Alexandra Ho. *New A* —3B **12**
Alexandra La. *Torq* —4C **20**
Alexandra Rd. *Daw* —4D **2**
Alexandra Rd. *New A* —3A **12**
Alexandra Rd. *Torq* —3C **20**
Alexandra Ter. *New A* —3H **11**
Alexandra Ter. *Teign* —5D **8**
Alexandra Ter. *Tot* —3F **31**
Alison Rd. *Paign* —2D **22**
Aller Brake Rd. *New A* —5B **12**
Aller Clo. *Kgswl* —1G **15**
Aller Hill. *Daw* —5B **2**
Aller Pk. Rd. *New A* —5B **12**
Aller Rd. *Kgswl* —1F **15**
All Hallows Rd. *Pres* —1F **23**
All Saints Rd. *Torq* —3D **20**
Alma Rd. *Brix* —2D **28**

Alpha Ter. *Tot* —3E **31**
Alpine Rd. *Torq* —4C **20**
Alston La. *Chur F* —5F **27**
Alta Vista Clo. *Teign* —2F **9**
Alta Vista Rd. *Paign* —1F **25**
Alwyns Clo. Teign —4E ***9***
(off Lwr. Brimley)
Anchorage Clo. *Brix* —2F **29**
Andor Av. *Kgstn* —4E **7**
Ansteys Clo. *Torq* —4F **21**
Anstey's Cove Rd. *Torq* —3F **21**
Anthea Rd. *Paign* —2C **22**
Antrim Ter. *Tot* —3F **31**
Anzac St. *Dart* —4C **30** (1A **30**)
Applegarth Av. *New A* —1D **10**
Applegarth Clo. *New A* —1D **10**
Apters Hill. Brix —2D ***28***
(off Middle St.)
Aqualand. —6C 20
Arch Cotts. *Kgstn* —4E **7**
Arch St. *Shal* —6C **8**
Archway Dri. *Dart* —3A **30**
Arden Dri. *Torq* —3G **19**
Argyle Ter. Tot —3E ***31***
(off Station Rd.)
Armada Cres. *Torq* —3F **19**
Armada Dri. *Teign* —1C **8**
Arran Clo. *Torq* —5D **16**
Arthington. *Torq* —2A **20**
Ashburn Clo. *Ashb* —4E **33**
Ashburn Gdns. *Ashb* —3F **33**
Ashburn Wlk. *Paign* —5E **25**
Ashburton By-Pass. *Ashb* —5E **33**
Ashburton Clo. *Bov T* —5A **4**
Ashburton Community Info. Point. —4E 33
Ashburton Mus. —4F 33
Ashburton Rd. *New A* —1A **10**
Ashburton Rd. *Tot* —2E **31**
Ashburton Rd. *Bov T* —5B **4**
Ashcombe Rd. *Daw* —1A **2**
Asheldon Rd. *Torq* —4F **21**
Ashfield Gdns. *Torq* —5H **19**
Ashfield Rd. *Torq* —4H **19**
Ash Hill. *Bish* —5H **9**
Ash Hill Rd. *Torq* —3B **20**
Ashleigh Clo. *Teign* —2D **8**
Ashleigh Clo. *Torq* —4E **17**
Ashleigh Ct. *Torq* —6E **21**
Ashleigh Dri. *Teign* —2D **8**
Ashleigh Gdns. *Dart* —4B **30**
Ashleigh Mt. *Teign* —2D **8**
Ashleigh Pk. *Teign* —2D **8**
Ashleigh Ri. *Teign* —2D **8**
Ashleigh Vs. Tot —4E ***31***
(off Plymouth Rd.)
Ashleigh Way. *Teign* —2D **8**
Ashley Priors La. *Torq* —3H **17**
Ashley Way. *Daw* —3E **3**
Ashmill Ct. *New A* —1E **11**
Ash Pk. *Holc* —1G **9**
Ashridge Gdns. *Kgstn* —5G **7**
Ash Rd. *Kgstn* —5F **7**
Ashton Ct. *Kgstn* —2F **7**
Ashton Ter. *Torq* —4F **21**
Ash Way. *New A* —4C **12**
Aspen Dri. *New A* —5C **12**
Aspen Way. *Paign* —2A **24**
Atherton La. *Tot* —4F **31**
Atway Clo. *Bov T* —2B **4**
Audley Av. *Torq* —1A **20**
Audley Ri. *New A* —4D **12**
Aveland Rd. *Torq* —2D **20**
Avenue Rd. *Kgswl* —2H **15**
Avenue Rd. *Torq* —3H **19**
Avenue Rd. *Bov T* —3B **4**
Avenue Ter. *Chur F* —2H **27**
Avenue, The. *New A* —2H **11**
Avery Hill. *Kgstn* —3F **7**
Avoca Av. *Torq* —3A **20**
Avon Rd. *Torq* —2E **19**

Babbacombe Downs Rd. *Torq* —1D **20**
Babbacombe Model Village. —1D 20
Babbacombe Rd. *Torq* —1D **20**
Babbage Rd. *Tot* —3F **31**
Back Rd. *New A* —2G **11**
(in two parts)
Badger Clo. *Dart* —3A **30**
Badger Clo. *Paign* —2C **22**
Badgers Clo. *Kgstn* —3E **7**
Badgers Way. *Bov T* —3C **4**
Badlake Clo. *Daw* —4C **2**
Badlake Hill. *Daw* —3C **2**
Bakers Hill. *Brix* —4D **28**
Bakers Hill. *New A* —2G **11**
Bakers Vw. *New A* —2F **11**
Bala Brook Clo. *Brix* —5A **28**
Balland Clo. *Ashb* —3G **33**
Balland La. *Ashb* —3G **33**
Balland Pk. *Ashb* —2G **33**
Balmoral Clo. *New A* —3B **12**
Bampfylde Rd. *Torq* —4A **20**
Bampton Clo. *Marl* —1A **22**
Banbury Pk. *Torq* —1F **19**
Bank La. *Brix* —2D **28**
Bank La. Tot —4F ***31***
(off Fore St.)
Bank St. *New A* —2G **11**
Bank St. *Teign* —5E **9**
Barchington Av. *Torq* —4E **17**
Barcombe Heights. *Pres* —3D **22**
Barcombe La. *Paign* —3E **23**
Barcombe Rd. *Pres* —3D **22**
Barewell Clo. *Torq* —1C **20**
Barewell Rd. *Torq* —1C **20**
Baring Courts. Tot —4G ***31***
(off Weston La.)
Barn Clo. Tot —3F ***31***
(off Station Rd.)
Barn Ct. *Chur F* —3H **27**
Barnfield. *Abbot* —1C **14**
Barnfield Clo. *Galm* —2F **27**
Barnfield Rd. *Brix* —4E **29**
Barnfield Rd. *Paign* —4C **22**
Barnfield Rd. *Torq* —1G **23**
Barnfield Ter. *Chur F* —2H **27**
Barnhay, The. *Sto G* —6A **24**
Barnhill Rd. *Kgswl* —3H **15**
Barn Owl Clo. *Torq* —4C **16**
Barn Pk. *Sto G* —5A **24**
Barn Pk. *Buckf* —5A **32**
Barn Pk. Clo. *Ippn* —5C **14**
Barnpark Clo. *Teign* —3E **9**
Barnpark Rd. *Teign* —4E **9**
Barnpark Ter. *Teign* —3E **9**
Barn Rd. *Paign* —3F **25**
Barns Clo. *Kgstn* —5F **7**
Barnsey Gdns. *Ashb* —2E **33**
Barnsfield La. *Buckf* —4A **32**
Barnsley Clo. *Teign* —4E **9**
Barnsley Dri. *Teign* —4E **9**
Barracks Hill. *Tot* —3E **31**
Barradon Clo. *Torq* —3F **17**
Barrington Rd. *Torq* —4F **21**
Bartlett M. *Torq* —5D **20**
Barton Av. *Paign* —5C **22**
Barton Clo. *Paign* —4C **22**
Barton Cres. *Daw* —4C **2**
Barton Cres. *Paign* —4C **22**
Barton Dri. *New A* —2E **11**
Barton Dri. *Paign* —4C **22**
Barton Gdns. *Paign* —4C **22**
Barton Hall Cvn. & Chalet Cen. *Torq* —4D **16**
Barton Hill. *Dac* —2F **17**
Barton Hill. *Daw* —4D **2**
Barton Hill Rd. *Torq* —6E **17**
Barton Hill Way. *Torq* —5D **16**
Barton La. *Daw* —4D **2**
Barton Rd. *Paign* —4C **22**
Barton Rd. *Torq* —1H **19**
Barton Ter. *Daw* —4D **2**
Barton Vs. *Daw* —4C **2**
Barum Clo. *Paign* —4F **23**
Bascombe Clo. *Chur F* —1G **27**
Bascombe Rd. *Chur F* —1F **27**
Bathill Camp Site. *Galm* —3D **26**
Bath La. *Torq* —4A **20**
Bath Ter. *Teign* —5E **9**
Batson Gdns. *Paign* —1D **24**
Batterways Rd. *Paign* —1B **24**
Battle Rd. *Heath* —4E **5**
Bayard's Cove. *Dart* —4C **30** (2B **30**)
Bayard's Cove Fort. —5C 30
Bayard's Hill. *Dart* —4C **30** (2B **30**)
Baymount Rd. *Paign* —4D **22**
Bay Vw. *Paign* —2G **23**
Bay Vw. Dri. *Teign* —3E **9**
Beach App. Brix —2E ***29***
(off Pump St.)
Beach Rd. *Daw W* —1H **3**
Beach Rd. *Paign* —5F **23**
Beach Rd. *Torq* —2E **21**
Beach St. *Daw* —4E **3**
Beacon Hill. *Torq* —6C **20**
Beacon La. *Kgswr* —5D **30**
Beacon Rd. *Kgswr* —5D **30**
Beal Farm M. *Chud* —1H **5**
Bearne's La. New A —2G ***11***
(off Market St.)
Beatty Way. *Dart* —2C **30**
Beaumont Clo. *Torq* —3G **19**
Beaumont Rd. *New A* —3H **11**
Beavers Brook Clo. *Pres* —1E **23**
Becket Rd. *Bov T* —3C **4**
Bedford Rd. *Torq* —1E **21**
Beech Dri. *Ippn* —5C **14**
Beechfield Av. *Torq* —5E **17**
Beechfield Pl. *Torq* —5E **17**
Beech Trees La. *Ippn* —5A **14**
Beechwood Av. *New A* —4B **12**
Beechwood Ct. *Teign* —2B **8**
Beenland Gdns. Torq —3A ***20***
(off East St.)
Beenland Pl. Torq —3A ***20***
(off East St.)
Belfield Av. *Marl* —1A **22**
Belfield Clo. *Marl* —6A **18**
Belfield Ri. *Marl* —6A **18**
Belfield Rd. *Paign* —4B **22**
Belfield Way. *Marl* —6A **18**
Belgrave Rd. *New A* —4C **12**
Belgrave Rd. *Torq* —4A **20**
Belgrave Ter. *Teign* —4E **9**
Belgravia Ter. *Kgswr* —4D **30**
Bella Vista Rd. *Brix* —1D **28**
Bellever Tor Dri. *Brix* —5A **28**
Belle Vue Rd. *Paign* —6F **23**
Bellrock Clo. *Torq* —4G **17**
Belmont Clo. *Kgstn* —2F **7**
Belmont Rd. *Brix* —3C **28**
Belmont Rd. *Torq* —3C **20**
Belmont Ter. *Tot* —3F **31**
Belvedere Rd. *New A* —6A **6**
Bench Tor Clo. *Torq* —1E **19**
Benedict Clo. *Teign* —2E **9**
Ben Jonson Clo. *Torq* —3G **19**
Ben Venue Clo. *Torq* —4D **20**
Berachah Rd. *Torq* —3C **20**
Berea Rd. *Torq* —3D **20**
Bere Cotts. *Daw* —3B **2**
Bere Hill. *Daw* —4B **2**
Berkeley Av. *Torq* —6B **16**
Berkeley Ri. *Torq* —6B **16**
Berry Av. *Paign* —5C **22**
Berry Clo. *Abbot* —1C **14**
Berry Ct. *Brix* —1F **29**
Berry Dri. *Paign* —5C **22**
Berry Head Country & Pk. Vis. Cen. —2H 29
Berry Head Fortifications. —2H 29
Berry Head Rd. *Brix* —2E **29**
Berry Hill. *Bish* —5G **9**
Berry La. *Kgstn* —4F **7**
Berry Mdw. *Kgstn* —5F **7**
Berry Rd. *Paign* —5C **22**
Berry Sq. Paign —5F ***23***
(off Beach Rd.)
Berrys Wood. *New A* —2E **11**
Besigheim Way. *New A* —2B **12**
Bethel Ter. Torq —4C ***20***
(off Princes Rd.)
Beverley Clo. *New A* —4F **11**
Beverley Gdns. *Ashb* —2G **33**
Beverley Pk. Cvn. Cen. *Good* —4E **25**
Beverley Ri. *Brix* —3C **28**
Beverley Way. *New A* —3F **11**
Bexley La. *Torq* —4A **20**
Bickford La. *Teign* —5E **9**
Bickley Rd. *Stone* —5D **14**
Bidwell Brook Dri. *Paign* —4E **25**
Bidwell Wlk. *Paign* —4E **25**
Bigadon La. *Buckf* —6C **32**
Bigbury Way. *Torq* —5G **17**
Biltor Rd. *Ippn* —6A **14**
Bingfield Clo. *Torq* —4D **20**
Birch Rd. *New A* —4C **12**
Birch Wlk. *Torq* —1F **19**
Birchwood Clo. *Tot* —4E **31**
Birdwood Ct. *Tot* —4F **31**
Bishops Av. *Bish* —6G **9**
Bishops Clo. *Torq* —5G **21**
Bishops Ct. *Bish* —5G **9**
Bishop's Pl. *Paign* —5E **23**
Bishops Ri. *Torq* —5H **21**
Bishopsteignton Ho. *Bish* —5F **9**
Bishopsteignton Mus. of Rural Life. —5H 9
Bishopsteignton Rd. *Teign* —5A **8**
Bishop's Wlk. *Torq* —3G **21**
Bishop Wilfrid Rd. *Teign* —3B **8**
Bitney La. *Abbot* —2D **14**
Bitton Av. *Teign* —4D **8**
Bitton Ct. *Teign* —4C **8**
Bitton Pk. Rd. *Teign* —4C **8**
(in two parts)
Blackball La. *Brix* —1D **28**
Blackberry Way. *Kgstn* —2F **7**
Blackbrook Av. *Paign* —4E **25**
Blackbrook Wlk. *Paign* —4E **25**
Blackenway La. *New A* —6E **13**
Blackhaven Clo. *Paign* —5E **25**
Blackpost La. *Tot* —4H **31**
Blackstone Rd. *Ippn* —6B **14**
Blackthorn Way. *Paign* —1A **24**
Bladon Clo. *New A* —4A **12**
Blagdon Rd. *Paign* —6A **22**
Blake Clo. *Torq* —1C **20**
Blakey Down La. *Paign* —2B **22**
Blatchcombe Dri. *Paign* —4C **22**
Blatchcombe Rd. *Paign* —4C **22**
Blenheim Clo. *New A* —1F **11**
Blenheim Clo. *Torq* —5F **21**
Blenheim Ter. *Bov T* —3B **4**
Bligh Clo. *Teign* —1C **8**
Blindwell Av. *Kgstn* —4F **7**
Blindwylle Rd. *Torq* —4H **19**
Blogishay La. *Ashb* —4F **33**
Blue Ball Hill. *Tot* —4F **31**

Blue Birchlea Ridge. *Bov T* —6B **4**
Blue Waters Dri. *Paign* —5F **25**
Blyths Wood Cres. *Torq* —2C **20**
Body Hayes Clo. *Sto G* —6A **24**
Bolton St. *Brix* —3D **28**
Bonair Clo. *Brix* —4D **28**
Bonds Mdw. *Bov T* —2B **4**
Borough Clo. *Paign* —2B **24**
Borough Pk. Rd. *Paign* —6A **22**
Borough Pk. Rd. *Tot* —3F **31**
Borough Rd. *Paign* —1A **24**
Borough Rd. *Torq* —6G **17**
Borthay Orchard. *Abbot* —6G **11**
Boscawen Pl. *Teign* —4D **8**
Bossell Pk. *Buckf* —5B **32**
Bossell Rd. *Buckf* —5B **32**
Bossell Ter. *Buckf* —4B **32**
Bottompark La. *Torq* —4E **17**
Bottoms La. *Dac* —3D **16**
Boundary Clo. *Kgswl* —1G **15**
Boundary Rd. *Torq* —4G **19**
Bourne Ct. *Brix* —5A **28**
Bourne Rd. *Kgswl* —2H **15**
Bourton La. *Tot* —3H **31**
Bourton Rd. *Tot* —3H **31**
Bourtons, The. *Tot* —2G **31**
Bove Pk. Rd. *Torq* —3F **17**
Bovey Tracey Rd. *New A* —4A **6**
Bowden Hill. *New A* —3H **11**
Bowden Hill. *Ashb* —5E **33**
Bowden Rd. *Ippn* —5C **14**
Bowerland Av. *Torq* —3E **17**
Bowland Clo. *Paign* —3D **24**
Boyds Dri. *Teign* —4E **9**
Bracken Clo. *New A* —4C **12**
Bracken Ri. *Paign* —1F **27**
Bradden Cres. *Brix* —3B **28**
Braddons Cliffe. *Torq* —5C **20**
Braddons Hill Rd. E. *Torq* —5C **20**
Braddons Hill Rd. W. *Torq* —5C **20**
Braddons St. *Torq* —5C **20**
Bradley Ct. *New A* —2G **11**
Bradley La. *New A* —2F **11**
Bradley Manor. —3E 11
Bradley Pk. Rd. *Torq* —1B **20**
Bradley Rd. *New A* —4F **11**
Bradley Rd. *Bov T* —2D **4**
Braeside Rd. *Paign* —1F **25**
Braeside Rd. *Torq* —3F **17**
Brake Houses. *New A* —3B **12**
Brakeridge Clo. *Chur F* —1F **27**
Bramble Clo. *Torq* —4G **19**
Branksome Clo. *Pres* —1F **23**
Branscombe Clo. *Torq* —3E **21**
Brantwood Clo. *Paign* —1D **24**
Brantwood Cres. *Paign* —2D **24**
Brantwood Dri. *Paign* —1D **24**
Breakneck Hill. *Teign* —1D **8**
Brendons Av. *Torq* —6F **19**
Brent Rd. *Paign* —5E **23**
*Brewery La. Brix —2D **28***
(off Market St.)
Briary La. *Torq* —4C **20**
Bridge Cft. *Ashb* —3E **33**
Bridge Rd. *Chur F* —2G **27**
Bridge Rd. *Kgswr* —1D **30**
Bridge Rd. *Shal* —6C **8**
Bridge Rd. *Torq* —4A **20**
Bridge St. *Ippn* —5B **14**
Bridge St. *Buckf* —4B **32**
Bridgetown. *Tot* —4G **31**
Bridgetown Ct. *Tot* —4G **31**
Bridgetown Hill. *Tot* —4G **31**
Bridgewater Gdns. *Tot* —4H **31**
Bridle Clo. *Paign* —5E **25**
Bridle Path, The. *Tot* —5F **31**
*Brim Brook Ct. Torq —1E **19***
(off Chinkwell Rise)
Brim Hill. *Maid* —1H **17**
Brimlands. *Brix* —3C **28**
Brimley Dri. *Teign* —4E **9**
Brimley Gdns. *Bov T* —5B **4**
Brimley Grange. *Bov T* —5A **4**
Brimley Halt. *Bov T* —5B **4**
Brimley La. *Bov T* —5A **4**
Brimley Pk. *Bov T* —5B **4**
Brimley Rd. *Bov T* —5A **4**
Brimley Va. *Bov T* —4B **4**
Briseham Clo. *Brix* —4E **29**
Briseham Rd. *Brix* —4E **29**
Britannia Av. *Dart* —4A **30**
Briwere Rd. *Torq* —2H **19**
Brixham Aquarium. —2E 29
Brixham Holiday Pk. *Brix* —1C **28**
Brixham Mus. —2D 28
Brixham Rd. *Kgswr* —4D **30**
Brixham Rd. *Paign* —1B **24**
Brixham Rd. *Brix* —2G **27**
Broadacre Dri. *Brix* —2E **29**
Broadgate Cres. *Kgswl* —3G **15**
Broadgate Rd. *Kgswl* —2G **15**
Broadlands. *Shal* —6C **8**
Broadlands Av. *New A* —2F **11**
Broadlands Ct. *New A* —2F **11**
Broadlands Rd. *Paign* —1D **24**
Broadley Dri. *Torq* —6F **19**
Broadmeade Ct. *New A* —3A **12**
Broadmeadow Ind. Est. *Teign* —4B **8**
Broadmeadow La. *Teign* —3A **8**
Broadmeadow Vw. *Teign* —4B **8**
Broad Oak Cres. *Tot* —4G **31**
Broadpark. *Bov T* —5A **4**
Broad Pk. *Ashb* —2F **33**
Broadpark Rd. *Paign* —3C **22**
Broadpark Rd. *Torq* —6F **19**
Broadpath. *Sto G* —6A **24**
(in two parts)
Broad Reach. *Paign* —6F **25**
Broadridge Clo. *New A* —1C **10**
Broadsands Av. *Paign* —6F **25**
Broadsands Bend. *Paign* —5F **25**
Broadsands Ct. *Paign* —6E **25**
Broadsands Pk. Rd. *Paign* —5F **25**
Broadsands Rd. *Paign* —6E **25**
Broadstone. *Dart* —3C **30** (1A **30**)
Broadstone Pk. Rd. *Torq* —6G **19**
Broadway Av. *Kgstn* —3E **7**
Broadway Rd. *Kgstn* —3D **6**
Bronescombe Av. *Bish* —5H **9**
Bronshill Rd. *Torq* —3C **20**
Brook Clo. *Holc* —1G **9**
Brookdale Clo. *Brix* —3C **28**
Brookdale Ct. *Brix* —3C **28**
Brookdale Pk. *Brix* —3C **28**
Brookdale Ter. *Daw* —4E **3**
Brookedor. *Kgswl* —2G **15**
Brookedor Gdns. *Kgswl* —2G **15**
Brookfield Clo. *Kgstn* —4F **7**
Brookfield Clo. *Paign* —3F **23**
Brookfield Dri. *Teign* —2E **9**
Brookfield Orchard. *Kgstn* —4F **7**
Brook Haven Clo. *Kgswl* —2G **15**
Brooklands. *Tot* —4H **31**
Brooklands La. *Torq* —5H **19**
Brook La. *Shal* —6B **8**
Brook Orchard. *Kgswl* —2G **15**
Brook Rd. *Ippn* —5B **14**
Brookside Clo. *Teign* —4C **8**
Brook St. *Daw* —4D **2**
Brookvale Clo. *Shal* —6B **8**
Brookvale Orchard. *Shal* —6B **8**
Brook Way. *Kgstn* —1E **7**
Broomborough Ct. *Tot* —4E **31**
Broom Clo. *Daw* —1F **3**
Broomhill Way. *Torq* —6D **16**
Broom Pk. *Torq* —4E **17**
Brownhill. *Heath* —4F **5**
Brownhills Rd. *New A* —2F **11**
Brownings End. *Ogwl* —4E **11**
Brownings Wlk. *Ogwl* —4E **11**
Browns Bri. Rd. *Torq* —6C **16**
Brown's Hill. *Dart* —1A **30**
Brunel Av. *Torq* —3G **17**
Brunel Clo. *Teign* —3E **9**
Brunel M. *Torq* —5H **19**
Brunel Rd. *New A* —2A **12**
Brunel Rd. *Paign* —6F **25**
Brunswick Pl. *Daw* —4D **2**
Brunswick Sq. *Torq* —3A **20**
Brunswick St. *Teign* —5E **9**
Brunswick Ter. *Torq* —3A **20**
*Brutus Cen. Tot —4F **31***
(off Station Rd.)
Buckeridge Av. *Teign* —3D **8**
Buckeridge Rd. *Teign* —2D **8**
Buckfast Abbey. —2C 32
Buckfast Butterflies. —4D 32
Buckfast Clo. *Buck* —3C **32**
Buckfastleigh Miniature Railway. —4D 32
Buckfast Rd. *Buck* —2C **32**
Buckland Brake. *New A* —3B **12**
Buckland Heights. *New A* —2C **12**
Buckland Rd. *New A* —3B **12**
(in three parts)
Buckland Vw. *New A* —1A **12**
Buck's Clo. *Bov T* —3C **4**
Budleigh Clo. *Torq* —3E **21**
Bullands Clo. *Bov T* —2B **4**
Buller Rd. *New A* —3H **11**
Bull Ring. *Ashb* —4F **33**
Bunting Clo. *New A* —4F **11**
Bunting Clo. *Teign* —3C **8**
Burch Gdns. *Daw* —1E **3**
Burdouns Way. *Kgstn* —1F **7**
Burke Rd. *Tot* —3G **31**
Burleigh Rd. *Torq* —2F **19**
Burnley Clo. *New A* —1C **10**
Burnley Rd. *New A* —1C **10**
Burn River Ri. *Torq* —1E **19**
Burnthouse Hill. *Kgswl* —6F **15**
Burridge Av. *Torq* —4G **19**
Burridge La. *Torq* —4B **20**
Burridge Rd. *Torq* —4G **19**
Burton Pl. *Brix* —3D **28**
Burton St. *Brix* —4D **28**
Burton Villa Clo. *Brix* —3D **28**
Bury Rd. *New A* —1G **11**
Bushell Rd. *New A* —1F **11**
Bushmead Av. *Kgswl* —2H **15**
Butland Av. *Paign* —2F **23**
Butland Rd. *Kgstn* —3E **7**
Buttercombe Clo. *Ogwl* —5E **11**
Butterlake. *Marl* —5A **18**
Butt's La. *New A* —5F **13**
Bygones Mus. —1D 20
Byron Rd. *Torq* —1B **20**
Byter Mill La. *Sto G* —6B **24**

Cabbage Hill. *Ashb* —5E **33**
Cadewell Cres. *Torq* —6C **16**
Cadewell La. *Torq* —1F **19**
Cadewell Pk. Rd. *Torq* —6B **16**
Cadwell Rd. *Paign* —4E **23**
Calvados Pk. *Kgstn* —4G **7**
Camborne Cres. *Paign* —5E **25**
Cambridge Rd. *Brix* —3B **28**
Cambridge Rd. *Torq* —6G **17**
Camden Rd. *Torq* —4C **20**
Camellia Clo. *Chur F* —1G **27**
Canada Hill. *Ogwl* —4E **11**
Canal Rd. *Kgstn* —5E **7**
Canal Way. *Kgstn* —5E **7**
Cannon Rd. *Heath* —4F **5**
Canons Clo. *Bish* —5G **9**
Captains Rd. *Kgstn* —3E **7**
Cardew Teapottery. —5C 4
Carew Gdns. *New A* —2C **12**
Carey Rd. *Dart* —4A **30**
Carhaix Way. *Daw* —2F **3**
Carleton Ct. *Paign* —3E **23**
Carlile Rd. *Brix* —2B **28**
Carlisle St. *New A* —2H **11**
Carlton Clo. *Pres* —1F **23**
Carlton Dri. *Pres* —1F **23**
Carlton Pl. *Teign* —5E **9**
Carlton Rd. *Torq* —3D **20**
Carlton Ter. *Daw* —4E **3**
Caroline Clo. *Kgswl* —4H **15**
*Carpenters Ct. New A —3H **11***
(off Church Rd.)
Carrions, The. *Tot* —4F **31**
Carswells. *Kgswl* —2G **15**
Cartwright Cres. *Teign* —3B **8**
Cary Av. *Torq* —2D **20**
Cary Castle Dri. *Torq* —1C **20**
Cary Pde. *Torq* —5C **20**
Cary Pk. *Torq* —2C **20**
Cary Pk. Rd. *Torq* —2D **20**
Cary Rd. *Paign* —2D **22**
Cary Rd. *Torq* —5B **20**
Cassiobury Way. *Torq* —5D **16**
Castle Cir. *Torq* —4B **20**
Castle Cir. Ct. *Torq* —4B **20**
Castle Ct. *Tot* —4E **31**
Castle La. *Comp* —3A **18**
Castle La. *Torq* —4C **20**
(in two parts)
Castle Rd. *Dart* —6D **30**
Castle Rd. *Kgswr* —5D **30**
Castle Rd. *Torq* —4B **20**
Castle St. *Tot* —3F **31**
Castle Way. *New A* —1D **10**
Castlewood Av. *New A* —6A **6**
Castor Clo. *Brix* —4E **29**
Castor La. *Good* —4E **25**
Castor Rd. *Brix* —4D **28**
Caunters Clo. *Ippn* —5B **14**
Cavalier Rd. *Heath & New A* —3E **5**
Cavendish Clo. *Daw* —3C **2**
Cavern Rd. *Brix* —3D **28**
Cavern Rd. *Torq* —4C **20**
Cecil Av. *Pres* —3E **23**
Cecilia Rd. *Paign* —2E **23**
Cecil Rd. *Paign* —5D **22**
Cedar Clo. *Teign* —2F **9**
Cedar Ct. Rd. *Torq* —2C **20**
Cedar Rd. *New A* —5C **12**
Cedar Rd. *Paign* —2F **23**
Cedars Rd. *Torq* —4D **20**
Cedars, The. *Tot* —3H **31**
Cedar Way. *Brix* —5B **28**
Centenary Way. *Torq* —5B **16**
Central Av. *Paign* —4E **23**
Centry Ct. *Brix* —3F **29**
Centry Rd. *Brix* —3F **29**
Century of Playtime Doll & Toy Mus. —5D 22
Chalfield Clo. *Torq* —4E **17**
Challabrook La. *Bov T* —4A **4**
Challycroft Rd. *Brix* —6B **28**
Chantry Clo. *Teign* —2F **9**
Chapel Ct. *Torq* —2A **20**
Chapel Ct. Yd. *Sto G* —5A **24**
Chapel Hill. *New A* —2G **11**
Chapel La. *Tot* —4G **31**
*Chapel La. Sto F —4C **30***
(off Newcomen Rd.)
Chapel La. *Dart* —2A **30**
Chapel of St Lawrence. —4F 33
(off St. Lawrence Lane)
Chapel Rd. *New A* —2A **12**
Chapel St. *Buckf* —4B **32**

Chapple Cross. *Bov T*—5A **4**
Chapple Rd. *Bov T*—4A **4**
Charlemont Rd. *Teign*—1D **8**
Charles Rd. *Kgswl*—5H **15**
Charles St. *Dart*—4C **30** (1A **30**)
Charlotte Clo. *Torq*—1A **20**
Charmouth Clo. *Torq*—3E **21**
Chartwell Clo. *Paign*—4B **22**
Chartwell Dri. *New A*—1F **11**
Chatsworth Rd. *Torq*—3C **20**
Chatto Rd. *Torq*—2B **20**
Chatto Way. *Torq*—2B **20**
Chelsea Pl. *Teign*—4D **8**
Chelston Rd. *New A*—1G **11**
Chelston Rd. *Torq*—6H **19**
Chercombe Bri. Rd. *New A* —2B **10**
Chercombe Clo. *New A*—1D **10**
Chercombe Valley Rd. *New A* —1D **10**
Cherry Brook Dri. *Paign*—5E **25**
Cherry Brook Sq. *Paign*—5E **25**
Cherry Brook Wlk. *Paign*—4E **25**
Cherry Cross. *Tot*—5F **31**
Cherry Gdns. *Paign*—4D **22**
Cherry Pk. Clo. *Torq*—1G **23**
Cherrywood Clo. *New A*—1D **10**
Chestnut Av. *Dart*—3A **30**
Chestnut Av. *Torq*—5A **20**
Chestnut Dri. *Brix*—5A **28**
Chestnut Dri. *Kgstn*—5G **7**
Chestnut Dri. *New A*—4D **12**
Chestnut Wlk. *Daw*—5C **2**
Chichester Way. *New A*—2B **12**
Chilcote Clo. *Torq*—1D **20**
Chiltern Clo. *Torq*—6G **19**
Chilton Av. *Teign*—3E **9**
Chinkwell Ri. *Torq*—1E **19**
Chiseldon Hill. *Brix*—5D **28**
Chiseldon La. *Brix*—6D **28**
Chockland Rd. *Kgstn*—2E **7**
Christina Pde. *Tot*—4H **31**
Christina Pk. *Tot*—4H **31**
Chudleigh Knighton Heath Nature Reserve. —1G 5
Chudleigh Rd. *Kgstn*—2D **6**
Chuley Hill. *Ashb*—5F **33**
Chuley Rd. *Ashb*—5F **33**
Church Clo. *Dart*—4C **30** (1B **30**)
Church Clo. *Ashtn*—4F **31**
Church Cotts. *Marl*—5A **18**
Church Ct. *Kgstn*—5F **7**
Church Ct. *New A*—2G **11**
Church Cross Rd. *Buck*—3B **32**
Church End Rd. *Kgswl*—2G **15**
Churchfields. *Dart*—4A **30**
Churchfields Dri. *Bov T*—3C **4**
Churchfields W. *Dart*—4A **30**
Church Hill. *Kgswr*—5D **30**
Church Hill. *Buckf*—3B **32**
Church Hill. *Marl*—5A **18**
Church Hill Cotts. *Marl*—6A **18**
Church Hill E. *Brix*—2D **28**
Church Hill W. *Brix*—2D **28**
Church Ho. Clo. *Chud*—1H **5**
Churchill Av. *Daw*—5D **2**
Churchill Dri. *Teign*—3E **9**
Churchills, The. *New A*—1F **11**
Church La. *Torq*—4A **20**
Church M. *Kgstn*—5F **7**
Church Path. *Ippn*—5A **14**
Church Path. *New A*—6B **6**
Church Path. *Paign*—5E **23**
Church Path. *Ashb*—4F **33**
Church Rd. *Bart*—4F **17**
Church Rd. *Bish*—5H **9**
Church Rd. *Dart & Sto F*—3A **30**
Church Rd. *New A*—3H **11**
Church Rd. *Ogwl*—4C **10**
Church Rd. *St M*—6G **17**
Church Rd. *Chur F*—2H **27**
Church St. *Brix*—2D **28**
Church St. *Daw*—4C **2**
Church St. *Kgstn*—5F **7**
Church St. *Paign*—5E **23**
Church St. *Torq*—4A **20**
Church St. *Buckf*—4B **32**
*Church Vw. Kgstn —5F **7***
(off Greenhill Rd.)
Church Vw. *Daw*—4C **2**
Church Wlk. *Sto G*—6A **24**
Churchward Rd. *Paign*—5E **23**
Church Way. *Kgswl*—2A **16**
(in two parts)
Church Way. *New A*—4B **12**
Church Way. *Torq*—2D **20**
Churscombe Grn. *Marl*—1B **22**
Churscombe Gro. *Marl*—1B **22**
Churscombe Pk. *Marl*—1A **22**
Churscombe Rd. *Marl*—1A **22**
Churston B'way. *Paign*—6E **25**
Churston Clo. *Galm*—2F **27**
Churston Rd. *Chur F*—3H **27**
Churston Way. *Brix*—3B **28**
Cistern St. *Tot*—4E **31**
Claddon La. *Maid*—2F **17**
Clampitt Clo. *Ippn*—6B **14**
*Clampitt La. Teign —5E **9***
(off Bank St.)
Clampitt Rd. *Ippn*—5B **14**
Clanage St. *Bish*—5G **9**
*Claradon M. Tot —4F **31***
(off Leechwell St.)
Claremont Av. *Kgswl*—3H **15**
Clarence Hill. *Dart* —4C **30** (1A **30**)
Clarence St. *Dart*—3C **30**
Clarendon Clo. *Torq*—3A **20**
Clarendon Ct. *Torq*—5D **20**
Clarendon Rd. *Ippn*—5B **14**
Clarendon Rd. *New A*—2G **11**
Claylands Dri. *Paign*—1C **24**
Clay La. *Teign*—4D **8**
Claypark Ter. *Sto G*—6B **24**
Cleaveland Ri. *Ogwl*—4E **11**
Clennon Av. *Paign*—1E **25**
Clennon Ct. *Torq*—5F **17**
Clennon Dri. *Paign*—1E **25**
Clennon Gdns. *Paign*—1E **25**
Clennon Heights. *Paign*—1E **25**
Clennon La. *Paign*—1D **24**
Clennon La. *Torq*—5F **17**
Clennon Pk. *Paign*—1E **25**
Clennon Ri. *Paign*—1E **25**
Clennon Summit. *Paign*—1E **25**
Cleveland Ct. *Paign*—6F **23**
*Cleveland Pl. Daw —4E **3***
(off Leigham Ct.)
*Cleveland Pl. Ogwl —4F **11***
(off Larksmead Way)
Cleveland Rd. *Paign*—6F **23**
Cleveland Rd. *Torq*—3A **20**
Cleve Ter. *Torq*—4F **21**
Cliff Ct. *Daw*—4E **3**
Cliffden Clo. *Teign*—4E **9**
Cliff Ho. *Paign*—6G **23**
Cliff M. *Paign*—6F **23**
Clifford Av. *Kgstn*—2E **7**
Clifford Clo. *Kgstn*—4F **7**
Clifford Clo. *Shal*—6C **8**
Clifford Dri. *Heath*—4E **5**
Clifford St. *Kgstn*—4F **7**
Cliff Pk. Av. *Paign*—2F **25**
Cliff Pk. Rd. *Paign*—3F **25**
Cliff Rd. *Paign*—6G **23**
Cliff Rd. *Teign*—2F **9**
Cliff Rd. *Torq*—1H **23**
Cliffside Rd. *Torq*—1D **20**
Clifton Bank. *Paign*—5D **22**
Clifton Clo. *Paign*—5C **22**
Clifton Cres. *Paign*—5D **22**
Clifton Gdns. *Paign*—5D **22**
Clifton Gro. *Paign*—5D **22**
Clifton Gro. *Torq*—5E **21**
Clifton Pl. *Daw*—4C **2**
Clifton Ri. *Paign*—5D **22**
Clifton Rd. *Paign*—5C **22**
Clifton Ter. *Torq*—5C **20**
Climsland Rd. *Paign*—6D **22**
Close, The. *Brix*—2C **28**
Close, The. *Daw*—1H **9**
Close, The. *Paign*—5F **25**
Clovelly Ri. *Daw*—5D **2**
Clovelly Ri. *Paign*—5B **22**
Clyst Av. *Brix*—5B **28**
Coach Pl. *New A*—3H **11**
Coach Rd. *New A*—4G **11**
Coastguard Cotts. *Daw*—4F **3**
Coastguard Cotts. *Torq*—6D **20**
*Coburg Pl. Torq —5C **20***
(off Melville St.)
Cockhaven Clo. *Bish*—6G **9**
Cockhaven Rd. *Bish*—6G **9**
Cockington Country Pk. & Vis. Cen. —5F 19
Cockington Court Gardens. —5F 19
Cockington La. *Torq*—3F **19**
Cockington La. *Pres*—2F **23**
Cockington Rd. *Marl*—6C **18**
Coffinswell La. *Kgswl*—3H **15**
Coker Av. *Torq*—3E **17**
Coldharbour. *Tot*—3H **31**
Coleman Av. *Teign*—3C **8**
Coleridge Ct. *Torq*—5F **17**
Cole's Ct. *Dart*—4C **30** (2B **30**)
Cole's La. *Kgswl*—2G **15**
Colin Rd. *Paign*—4F **23**
Collaford La. *Dart*—1A **30**
Collapark. *Tot*—4E **31**
Collaton Ct. *Torq*—1F **19**
Collaton Rd. *Torq*—6A **16**
College. *Bov T*—2D **4**
College Rd. *New A*—4G **11**
College Way. *Dart*—3B **30**
Colleybrook Clo. *Kgstn*—1E **7**
Colley Cres. *Paign*—5D **22**
Colley End Pk. *Paign*—5D **22**
Colley End Rd. *Paign*—5B **22**
Collingwood Clo. *Torq*—6D **20**
Collingwood Clo. *Town I*—4A **30**
*Collingwood Ind. Est. Dart —3A **30***
(off Collingwood Rd.)
Collingwood Rd. *Paign*—6D **22**
Collingwood Rd. *Town I*—4A **30**
Collins Rd. *Tot*—3E **31**
Colston Rd. *Buckf*—5D **32**
Colwyn Ct. *Torq*—4F **21**
Combe Bank. *Brix*—3C **28**
Combe La. *Galm*—5E **27**
Combe Rd. *Torq*—5G **17**
*Commanders Cut. Dart —3B **30***
(off Flagstaff Rd.)
Commercial Rd. *Daw*—4E **3**
Commercial Rd. *Paign*—5E **23**
Common La. *Kgswl*—4E **15**
Commons La. *Daw*—3D **2**
Commons La. *Shal*—6B **8**
Commons Old Rd. *Shal*—6C **8**
(in two parts)
Compton Castle. —3A 18
Compton Pl. *Torq*—6G **17**
Condor Dri. *Torq*—5C **16**
Congella Rd. *Torq*—3D **20**
Conifers, The. *Torq*—4G **17**
Coniston Clo. *Brix*—5B **28**
Coniston Ct. *Paign*—1D **24**
Coniston Rd. *Ogwl*—5E **11**
Conniford La. *Ippn*—6A **14**
Connybear La. *New A*—6E **13**
Conway Cres. *Paign*—6D **22**
Conway Rd. *Paign*—6D **22**
Cooke Dri. *Ippn*—5C **14**
Cooks Clo. *Kgstn*—4G **7**
Cooks Clo. *Ashb*—3G **33**
Cook Way. *Brix*—5C **28**
Coombe Av. *Teign*—4C **8**
Coombe Clo. *Dart*—3C **30**
Coombe Clo. *Bov T*—3D **4**
Coombe Cross. *Bov T*—3D **4**
*Coombe Gdns. Teign —4C **8***
(off First Av.)
Coombe La. *Torq*—6F **17**
Coombe La. *Bov T*—3D **4**
Coombe La. *Teign*—2C **8**
(Paddons La.)
Coombe La. *Teign*—3A **8**
(Radway St., in two parts)
Coombe Mdw. *Bov T*—3D **4**
Coombe Pk. Cotts. *Torq*—6F **17**
Coombe Pk. Rd. *Teign*—3C **8**
Coombe Rd. *Dart*—3C **30**
Coombe Rd. *Paign*—2E **23**
Coombe Rd. *Shal*—6A **8**
Coombesend Rd. *Kgstn*—4G **7**
(in two parts)
Coombesend Rd. E. *Kgstn*—4H **7**
Coombeshead Rd. *New A*—1E **11**
Coombe Shute. *Sto G*—6A **24**
Coombe, The. *Dart*—3C **30**
Coombe, The. *Galm*—2E **27**
Coombe Va. Rd. *Teign*—3C **8**
Coombe Vw. *Teign*—2B **8**
Copland La. *Tot*—3E **31**
Copland Meadows. *Tot*—3E **31**
Copley Clo. *Paign*—5C **22**
*Cop Path. Daw —5C **2***
(off Taylor Clo.)
Copperwood Clo. *Ashb*—4E **33**
Coppice, The. *Daw*—6D **2**
Copse, The. *New A*—3D **12**
Copythorne Clo. *Brix*—3B **28**
Copythorne Pk. *Brix*—3B **28**
Copythorne Rd. *Brix*—2H **27**
Corfe Cres. *Torq*—1A **20**
Cormorant Clo. *Torq*—4C **16**
Cornacre Clo. *Torq*—2F **19**
Cornacre Rd. *Torq*—2F **19**
*Cornfield Grn. Torq —5G **17***
(off Roberts Clo.)
Corn Pk. Rd. *Abbot*—1B **14**
Coronation Av. *Daw*—5D **2**
Coronation Rd. *Kgstn*—4F **7**
Coronation Rd. *New A*—2F **11**
Coronation Rd. *Tot*—3F **31**
Coronation St. *Shal*—6C **8**
Corsham Rd. *Paign*—6D **22**
Coryton Clo. *Daw*—4D **2**
Cotmore Clo. *Brix*—5B **28**
Cotswold Clo. *Torq*—6G **19**
Cottey Mdw. *Kgstn*—5F **7**
Courtenay Gdns. *New A*—3H **11**
Courtenay Pk. *New A*—2A **12**
*Courtenay Pl. Teign —5E **9***
(off Triangle Pl.)
Courtenay Rd. *New A*—3G **11**
Courtenay Rd. *Paign*—3F **25**
Courtenay St. *New A*—2G **11**
Courtfield. *Tot*—4H **31**
Court Ga. Clo. *Ippn*—6A **14**
Courtland Rd. *Paign*—4E **23**
Courtland Rd. *Torq*—2E **19**
Courtlands Rd. *New A*—3A **12**
Court Rd. *Abbot*—1B **14**
Court Rd. *Torq*—4F **19**
Cousens Clo. *Daw*—2F **3**

Coventry Farm Trad. Est. Kgswl —5H 15
Coverdale Rd. Paign —5E 23
Cranford Rd. Paign —2D 22
Creek Rd. Dart —3A 30
Crescent Ct. Dart —4A 30 (off Townstal Cres.)
Cresswell Clo. Kgswl —2H 15
Cresta's. Torq —3D 20
Crest Hill. Buckf —4B 32
Crest Vw. Paign —6F 23
Cricket Fld. Rd. New A —1H 11
Cricketfield Rd. Torq —2H 19
Cricket La. Buckf —3A 32
Croft Clo. Ogwl —4C 10
Croft Hill. Torq —4B 20
Croft Mdw. Ippn —5B 14
Croft Orchard. Ippn —5B 14
Croft Rd. Ippn —5B 14
Croft Rd. Ogwl —4B 10
Croft Rd. Torq —4B 20
Croker's Mdw. Bov T —2B 4
Crokers Way. Ippn —5B 14
Cromwells Way. Bov T —2B 4
Cross Grange Trad. Est. Heath —3E 5
Cross Hill. New A —2F 13
Cross La. New A —1G 13
Crossley Moor Rd. Kgstn —4F 7
Cross Pk. Brix —4C 28
Cross Pk. Neth —1G 13
Cross Pk. Tot —3H 31
Crosspark Av. Torq —1F 19
Crossparks. Dart —5A 30 (in two parts)
Crossway. Good —3F 25
Crossways Shop. Cen., The. Paign —5E 23 (off Hyde Rd.)
Crown & Anchor Way. Paign —5E 23
Crownhill Ct. Torq —3H 19
Crownhill Cres. Galm —2E 27
Crownhill Pk. Torq —3H 19
Crownhill Ri. Torq —3H 19
Crownley La. Sto G —5A 24
Crown Sq. Shal —6C 8
Crowther's Hill. Dart —4C 30 (2A 30)
Crystal Clo. Paign —3F 25
Cudhill Rd. Brix —3C 28
Culm Clo. Torq —1E 19
Culverdale. Tot —5H 31
Culvery Grn. Torq —1E 19
Cumber Clo. Brix —2C 28
Cumber Dri. Brix —2C 28
Cumberland Grn. Brix —2C 28
Curledge St. Paign —6E 23
Custom Ho. Hill. Teign —5D 8
Cypress Clo. Torq —4B 20

Daccabridge Rd. Kgswl —3G 15
Daccombe Hill. Dac —3D 16
Daccombe Mill La. Kgswl —3H 15
Daddyhole Rd. Torq —6D 20
Daggers Copse. New A —2E 11
Dagmar St. Shal —6C 8
Dagra La. Shal —6A 8
Daimonds La. Teign —4D 8
Dainton M. Paign —6E 23
Dairy Hill. Torq —2F 19
Daison Cotts. Torq —2B 20
Daison Cres. Torq —1C 20
Dalverton Ct. Brix —1D 28
Danby Heights Clo. Torq —5F 21
Danvers Rd. Torq —5E 17
Daphne Clo. Torq —5E 21
Darran Clo. Kgstn —4G 7
Darran Rd. Kgstn —4G 7
Dart Av. Torq —1F 19
Dart Bri. Rd. Buckf —4C 32
Dartington La. Tot —2E 31
Dartmoor Otter Sanctuary. —4D 32
Dartmouth Mus. —4C 30 (1B 30)
Dartmouth Rd. Paign —5E 23
Dartmouth Rd. Chur F —1E 27
Dartmouth St Saviour's Church. —4C 30 (1B 30)
Darton Gro. Sto G —6A 24
Dartside. Tot —2E 31
Dartside Ct. Dart —3C 30 (off Clarence St.)
Dart Vw. Rd. Galm —1E 27
Dart Vs. Tot —5F 31
Dashpers. Brix —4C 28
David Rd. Paign —4D 22
Davies Av. Paign —5D 24
Davis Av. Torq —3G 19
Davis Ct. New A —1F 11
Davis Rd. Dart —4A 30
Dawes Clo. Ogwl —5E 11
Dawlish Rd. Teign —4E 9
Dawlish St. Teign —4E 9
Dawlish Warren Rd. Daw —1H 3
Daws Mdw. Kgstn —5F 7
Deans Clo. Bish —5G 9
Decoy Country Pk. —4H 11
Decoy Ind. Est. New A —5A 12
Decoy Rd. New A —3A 12
Deep Dene Clo. Brix —4B 28
Deep, The. —2E 29 (off The Quay)
Deer Pk. Av. Teign —3C 8
Deer Pk. Clo. Teign —3C 8
Deer Pk. Dri. Teign —3C 8
Deerpark La. New A —6G 13
Deer Pk. Rd. New A —4A 12
Deers Leap Clo. Pres —1E 23
Den Brook Clo. Torq —3E 21
Denbury Rd. New A & Ogwl —6C 10
Den Cres. Teign —5E 9
Dendy Rd. Paign —5E 23
Den Promenade. Teign —5E 9
Den Rd. Teign —5E 9
Den, The. Teign —5E 9
Denys Rd. Torq —3D 20
Denys Rd. Tot —4F 31
Derncleugh Gdns. Daw —1H 9
Derrell Rd. Paign —1D 24
Derwent Rd. Torq —2C 20
De Tracey Pk. Bov T —3C 4
Devondale Chalet Pk. Daw W —1H 3
Devondale Ct. Daw W —1H 3
Devon Heath. Chud —1H 5
Devon Ho. Dri. Bov T —2D 4
Devon Ho. Flats. Bov T —2D 4
Devon Sq. New A —2H 11
Devons Rd. Torq —2D 20
Devon Ter. Tot —4G 31
Devon Valley Holiday Village. Shal —6A 8
Dickers Ter. Kgstn —4F 7
Diptford Clo. Paign —2B 24
Dixon Clo. Paign —2B 22
Dobbin Arch. Kgswl —3G 15
Doctors Rd. Brix —4D 28
Dolbeare Rd. Ashb —3G 33 (in two parts)
Dolphin Ct. Shal —6C 8
Dolphin Ct. Rd. Paign —2C 22
Dolphin Cres. Paign —2C 22
Dolphin Holiday Cen. Brix —4E 29
Dorchester Gro. Torq —6E 17
Dornafield Clo. Ippn —5B 14
Dornafield Dri. E. Ippn —5B 14
Dornafield Dri. W. Ippn —5B 14
Dornafield Rd. Ippn —5B 14
Dosson Gro. Torq —2H 19
Doughy La. Den —6A 10
Douglas Av. Brix —3F 29
Douglas Ho. Teign —4D 8 (off Bitton Pk. Rd.)
Dower Ct. Paign —3F 23
Dower Rd. Torq —2B 20
Downaway La. Dac —1D 16
Downfield Clo. Brix —4B 28
Drake Av. Teign —1C 8
Drake Av. Torq —3F 19
Drake Dri. Good —3D 24
Drake La. Bov T —3D 4
Drake Rd. New A —2C 12
Drake Rd. Bov T —3D 4
Drakes Rd. Paign —1B 24
Drew's Fld. La. Comp —2A 18
Drew St. Brix —4D 28
Drive, The. Bish —5F 9
Drive, The. Brix —5D 28
Drive, The. Daw —4E 3
Drum Way. Heath —4E 5
Duce Pl. Teign —3E 9
Duchy Av. Pres —1D 22
Duchy Dri. Pres —1D 22
Duchy Gdns. Pres —6D 18
Duchy Pk. Pres —1D 22
Duckspond Rd. Buckf —5A 32
Dukes Clo. Paign —5B 22
Dukes Rd. Tot —5H 31
Duke St. Dart —4C 30 (1A 30)
Dulverton M. Paign —3B 22
Duncannon La. Sto G —6A 24
Duncannon Mead. Sto G —6A 24
Dunmere Rd. Torq —3C 20
Dunmore Ct. Shal —6D 8
Dunmore Dri. Shal —6D 8
Dunning Rd. Teign —2C 8
Dunning Wlk. Teign —3C 8 (off Lake Av.)
Dunstone Clo. Paign —2B 22
Dunstone Pk. Rd. Paign —2B 22
Dunstone Ri. Paign —2B 22
Durham Clo. Paign —2E 23
Durleigh Rd. Brix —3C 28

Eagle Clo. Kgstn —1E 7
Eaglewood Clo. Torq —5B 16
Earls Ct. Torq —3A 20
Earls Wood Dri. Paign —4A 22
E. Cliff. Teign —4E 9
E. Cliff Clo. Daw —3E 3
E. Cliff Gdns. Daw —3E 3
E. Cliff Rd. Daw —3E 3
E. Cliff Wlk. Teign —4F 9
East End Ter. Ashb —2G 33
Easterfield La. Torq —5G 17
Eastern Esplanade. Paign —6F 23
Eastern Rd. Ashb —3G 33
E. Pafford Av. Torq —5G 17
East St. Den —6A 10
East St. Ippn —5B 14
East St. New A —2G 11
East St. Torq —3A 20
East St. Bov T —2C 4
East St. Ashb & Bov T —4F 33
Eastwood Cres. New A —1D 10
Eaton Ct. Teign —2D 8
Eaton Hill Dri. Dart —3B 30 (off Flagstaff Rd.)
Eaton Pl. Paign —6E 23
Ebenezer Rd. Paign —6D 22
Eden Clo. Brix —4D 28
Eden Gro. Paign —4C 22
Eden Pk. Brix —4D 28
Edenvale Rd. Paign —3C 22
Edgelands La. Ippn —6A 14
Edgeley Rd. Torq —5F 17
Edginswell Clo. Torq —6B 16
Edginswell La. Kgswl & Torq —4G 15
Edinburgh Rd. Brix —4E 29
Edinburgh Vs. Torq —3A 20
Egerton Rd. Torq —3D 20
Elba Clo. Paign —4F 25
Elberry La. Paign & Chur F —6G 25
Elizabeth Av. Brix —6B 28
Elizabeth Ct. Torq —4A 20
Elizabeth Ct. Tot —4H 31 (off Furze Rd.)
Elizabeth Sq. New A —3C 12
Elkin's Hill. Brix —2E 29
Ellacombe Chu. Rd. Torq —3C 20
Ellacombe Rd. Torq —3C 20
Ellesmere. Torq —5D 20
Ellesmere Rd. Torq —4F 21
Elliot Plain. Buckf —4C 32
Elliott Gro. Brix —3B 28
Elmbank. Buckf —5A 32
Elmbank Gdns. Paign —6D 22
Elmbank Rd. Paign —6D 22
Elm Dri. Kgstn —4F 7
Elm Gro. Teign —1D 8
Elm Gro. Clo. Daw —3E 3
Elm Gro. Dri. Daw —3E 3
Elm Gro. Rd. Daw —2E 3
Elmhirst Dri. Tot —4H 31
Elmhurst Ct. Teign —4D 8
El Monte Clo. Teign —3D 8
Elm Pk. Paign —5C 22
Elm Rd. Brix —5B 28
Elm Rd. New A —2H 11
Elmsleigh Pk. Paign —6E 23
Elmsleigh Rd. Paign —6E 23
Elm Wlk. Tot —4H 31
Elmwood Av. New A —1D 10
Elmwood Cres. Daw —3E 3
Elsdale Rd. Paign —1D 24
Embankment, The. Shal —6B 8
Emblett Dri. New A —1D 10
Emblett Hill Vw. Ogwl —4E 11
Embury Clo. Kgswl —3H 15
Emlyn Pl. Bov T —3C 4
Emmetts Pk. Ashb —3G 33
Emmetts Pl. Abbot —1C 14
Empire Ct. Torq —2B 20
Empire Rd. Torq —2B 20
Empsons Clo. Daw —4C 2
Empsons Hill. Daw —4C 2
Enfield Rd. Torq —2D 20
English Riviera Cen. Torq —5A 20
Erica Dri. Torq —4E 17
Esplanade. Teign —5E 9
Esplanade Ct. Paign —5F 23
Esplanade Rd. Paign —6F 23
Esplanade, The. Dart —2C 30
Eugene Rd. Paign —3F 23
Eureka Ter. Bov T —2C 4
Eveleigh Clo. Brix —4D 28
Exe Hill. Torq —1E 19
Exeter Av. Torq —6E 17
Exeter Rd. Daw —4E 3
Exeter Rd. Kgstn —1E 7
Exeter Rd. New A —5B 6
Exeter Rd. Teign —2C 8
Exeter St. Teign —4D 8

Factory Row. Torq —4B 20
Fairfax Pl. Dart —4C 30 (2B 30)
Fairfax Rd. Heath —3E 5
Fairfield Clo. Bov T —3B 4
Fairfield Rd. Kgswl —4H 15
Fairfield Rd. Torq —1A 20

Fairfield Ter. New A —2H 11
Fairies Hill. Buck —3C 32
Fair Isle Clo. Torq —5D 16
Fairlea Clo. Daw —1F 3
Fairlea Rd. Daw —2E 3
Fairview Rd. Dart —4B 30 (1A 30)
Fairview Rd. Den —6A 10
Fairwater Clo. Kgstn —4G 7
Fairwaters. Kgstn —3F 7
Fairway Clo. Chur F —2G 27
Fairy La. Buckf —5A 32
Falkland Dri. Kgstn —3G 7
Falkland Rd. Torq —5A 20
Falkland Way. Teign —2C 8
Falloway Clo. Torq —5F 17
Fallowfield Clo. New A —2C 12
Falmouth Clo. Torq —1E 19
Farm Clo. Kgswl —1G 15
Farmyard La. Comp —3A 18
Farthing La. Marl —1A 22
Farwell Rd. Tot —4E 31
Faulkner Clo. Dart —4A 30
Fay Rd. Daw —4E 3
Fern Clo. Brix —3E 29
Ferncombe Clo. Kgstn —1F 7
Ferncombe Dri. Kgstn —1F 7
Ferndale. Dart —4B 30 (2A 30)
Ferndale Rd. Teign —3D 8
Ferndale Rd. Torq —2E 19
Fernham Ter. Paign —4E 23
Fernicombe Rd. Paign —4B 22
Fern Rd. New A —5C 12
Fernworthy Clo. Torq —2D 18
Ferrers Grn. Chur F —3H 27
Field Clo. Pres —1E 23
Firbank Rd. Daw —1F 3
Firestone La. New A —6F 11
Firlands Rd. Torq —5F 17 (in two parts)
Firleigh Rd. Kgstn —2E 7
First Av. Daw —5C 2
First Av. Teign —4C 8
First Av. Torq —1B 20
First Dri. Teign —3F 9 (Dawlish Rd.)
First Dri. Teign —4D 8 (Exeter Rd.)
Fir Wlk. Torq —1F 19
Fishacre Clo. Paign —3B 22
Fishchowter's La. Tot —5E 31
Fishcombe Rd. Brix —1C 28
Fisher Rd. New A —2G 11
Fisher St. Paign —6D 22
Five Lanes Rd. Marl —1A 22
Flagstaff Rd. Dart —3B 30
Flavel Pl. Dart —1B 30
Flavel St. Dart —1A 30
Fleet St. Torq —5C 20
Fleet Wlk. Torq —5C 20 (off Fleet St.)
Fleet Wlk. Shop. Cen. Torq —5C 20
Fletcher Clo. Torq —2H 19
Flete Av. New A —3C 12
Flete Clo. New A —3C 12
Flood St. Sto G —5A 24
Florence Pl. New A —3A 12
Florida Rd. Torq —4D 20
Flow La. Bish —6G 9 (in two parts)
Fluder Cres. Kgswl —4A 16
Fluder Hill. Kgswl —3H 15
Fluder La. Dac —2E 17
Fluder Ri. Kgswl —4A 16
Follafield Pk. Brix —5C 28
Football La. Kgstn —3F 7
Footland La. Dac —2D 16
Footlands Rd. Paign —1D 24
Forbes Clo. Heath —4E 5
Ford. Dart —4B 30 (in two parts)
Forde Clo. Abbot —6F 11
Forde Clo. New A —2A 12
Fordens La. Holc —1G 9
Forde Pk. New A —3A 12
Forder La. Bish —5F 9 (in two parts)
Forde Rd. New A —2A 12
Ford Pk. Chud —1H 5
Ford Rd. Abbot —6G 11
Ford Rd. Tot —3G 31
Ford Valley. Dart —4B 30
Foredown La. Kgswl —3F 15
Foresters Ter. Teign —5D 8
Fore St. Bart —4E 17
Fore St. Bish —5G 9
Fore St. Brix —2D 28
Fore St. Dart & Kgswr —4D 30
Fore St. Ippn —5B 14
Fore St. Kgswl —3G 15
Fore St. Kgstn —4F 7
Fore St. Shal —6C 8
Fore St. St M —1C 20 (in two parts)
Fore St. Teign —4D 8 (in two parts)
Fore St. Tot —4F 31
Fore St. Bov T —3C 4
Fore St. Buckf —4B 32
Forest Ridge Rd. Paign —2C 22
Forest Rd. Torq —3B 20
Forgeway Clo. Torq —5G 19
Fortescue Rd. Paign —2F 23
Fortune Way. Torq —2C 20
Foss Slip. Dart —1A 30
Foss St. Dart —4C 30 (1A 30)
Fouracre Way. Kgstn —3G 7
Fourth Av. Teign —3C 8
Fowey Av. Torq —1E 19
Foxhole Rd. Paign —5B 22
Foxhole Rd. Torq —5G 19
Foxhollows. New A —3D 12
Foxlands Wlk. St M —1D 20 (off Wolborough St.)
Foxley Cres. New A —2E 11
Fox Tor Clo. Paign —6E 25
Franeth Clo. Kgstn —3F 7
Fraser Dri. Teign —3C 8
Frederick Ter. Daw —4D 2 (off Stockton Rd.)
Freestone Rd. Kgstn —3E 7
French St. Teign —4E 9
Freshwater Dri. Paign —5D 24
Frobisher Clo. Teign —1C 8
Frobisher Grn. Torq —3F 19
Frobisher Way. Good —3E 25
Froude Av. Torq —3G 17
Fullaford Pk. Buckf —5A 32
Fulton Clo. Ippn —5B 14
Furlong Clo. Buck —2B 32
Furness Clo. Paign —3D 24
Furrough Ct. Torq —1D 20
Furrough Cross. Torq —1D 20
Furze Cap. Kgstn —1E 7
Furzedown Rd. Kgswl —2H 15
Furzegood. Marl —1A 22
Furzeham Ct. Brix —2C 28
Furzeham Pk. Brix —2D 28
Furzehill Rd. Torq —3B 20
Furze La. Brix —2E 29
Furzeleigh La. Bov T —2B 4
Furze Rd. Tot —4H 31

Gabwell La. Torq —1G 17
Gainsborough Clo. Torq —5E 21
Gales Crest. Chud —1H 5
Galloway Dri. Teign —2B 8
Galmpton Ct. Galm —2E 27 (off Galmpton Farm Clo.)
Galmpton Farm Clo. Galm —2E 27
Galmpton Glade. Galm —2E 27
Galmpton Holiday Pk. Galm —3E 27
Gard Clo. Torq —4F 17
Garden Rd. Elcm —3C 20
Garfield Rd. Paign —5F 23
Garlic Rea. Brix —2E 29 (in two parts)
Garners Clo. Ogwl —4C 10
Garners La. Ogwl —4C 10
Garrow Clo. Brix —4D 28
Garston Av. New A —1G 11
Garth Rd. Torq —5F 17
Gatehouse Clo. Daw —3D 2
Gatehouse Hill. Daw —3E 3
Gatehouse Ri. Daw —3E 3
Gate Tree Clo. Kgstn —4G 7
Gattery La. Brix —6A 28
Gaze Hill. New A —6A 6
George Rd. Paign —2E 23
George St. New A —2G 11
George St. Teign —5E 9
Georgian Ct. Torq —3F 21
Gerston Pl. Paign —5E 23
Gerston Rd. Paign —5E 23
Gerstons, The. Paign —5E 23
Gestridge Rd. Kgstn —3E 7
Gibson Dri. Paign —4D 24
Gibson Gdns. Paign —4D 24
Gibson Rd. Paign —4D 24
Gilbert Av. Teign —2C 8
Gilbert Clo. Torq —3G 19
Gilbert Rd. New A —2B 12
Gilbert Way. Good —3D 24
Gillard Rd. Brix —3F 29
Gilpin Clo. Daw —2F 3
Gipsy La. Buckf —6A 32
Gladstone Pl. New A —2H 11
Gladstone Ter. Teign —4E 9
Glebe Clo. New A —2E 11
Glebelands. Buckf —3A 32
Glebeland Way. Torq —1E 19
Glebe, The. Ippn —5A 14
Glencarnock Clo. Torq —2H 19
Glendaragh Rd. Teign —4E 9
Glenmore Rd. Brix —3D 28
Glen Rd. Paign —4E 23
Glenside Clo. Teign —3D 8
Glen, The. New A —3C 12
Glenthorne Clo. Torq —5E 21
Gloucester Clo. Torq —6E 17
Gloucester Rd. New A —3H 11
Gloucester Rd. Teign —4D 8
Godfrey Av. Pres —1E 23
Golden Clo. Brix —5C 28
Golden Hind, The. —2E 29
Golden Pk. Av. Torq —4E 17
Golden Sands Holiday Pk. Daw W —1G 3
Golden Ter. Daw —4D 2
Gollands. Brix —2B 28
Gollands Clo. Brix —2B 28
Golvers Hill Rd. Kgstn —4F 7
Goodridge Clo. Daw —2E 3
Goodrington Holiday Cen. Good —1F 25
Goodrington Rd. Paign —4D 24
Goodstone Way. Paign —2C 24
Gorway. Teign —3E 9
Goshen Rd. Torq —4H 19
Gothic Rd. New A —3G 11
Gourders La. Kgswl —5G 15
Grafton Rd. Torq —5C 20
Grafton Rd. New A —2G 11
Grafton Ter. Torq —5C 20
Graham Rd. Paign —2D 22
Grandison Av. Bish —5H 9
Grand Pier, The. —5E 9
Grange Av. Paign —3E 25
Grange Clo. Ippn & New A —4A 12
Grange Ct. Holiday Cen. Good —2E 25
Grange Dri. Teign —3D 8
Grange Heights. Paign —3D 24
Grange Heights Clo. Paign —4D 24
Grange Pk. Bish —5F 9
Grange Pk. Cvn. Pk. Abbot —1B 14
Granger Clo. Dart —3A 30
Grange Rd. Abbot —1C 14
Grange Rd. Paign —4D 24
Grange Rd. Torq —4D 20 (in two parts)
Grange Rd. Buck —2A 32
Grange Vw. Abbot —1C 14
Grange Vw. Paign —3D 24
Grasmere Clo. Torq —5G 17
Gt. Bridge. Ashb —3E 33
Gt. Furlong. Bish —5F 9
Great Gate. Brix —3D 28
Gt. Headland Cres. Paign —2F 23
Gt. Headland Rd. Paign —2F 23
Gt. Hill Rd. Torq —3E 17
Greatpark La. Paign —5A 22
Gt. Parks Rd. Paign —6B 22
Gt. Rea Rd. Brix —2E 29
Gt. Tor Clo. Paign —2C 22
Gt. Western Clo. Paign —1E 25
Gt. Western Rd. Paign —5E 23
Greebys, The. Paign —5D 22
Greenaway Rd. Cof —6E 13
Greenaway Rd. New A —1F 11
Greenaway Vs. New A —1G 11
Greenbank Av. Kgstn —4E 7
Greenbank Rd. Brix —3C 28
Greenfield Rd. Paign —1D 22
Greenhill. Kgstn —5F 7
Greenhill Gdns. Kgswl —3G 15
Greenhill La. Den —6A 10
Greenhill Rd. Kgswl —3G 15
Greenhill Rd. Kgstn —5F 7
Greenhill Way. Kgstn —5E 7
Greenlands Av. Paign —5C 22
Green La. Chur F —2H 27
Greenover Clo. Brix —4C 28
Greenover Rd. Brix —4C 28
Green Pk. Rd. Paign —2C 22
Green Pk. Wlk. Paign —2C 22
Greenswood Rd. Brix —4D 28
Green, The. Shal —6C 8
Greenway Clo. Torq —6F 17
Greenway Gdns. Torq —5F 17
Greenway La. St M —1C 20
Greenway Pk. Galm —3E 27
Greenway Rd. Chel —5G 19
Greenway Rd. Galm —5B 26
Greenway Rd. St M —1C 20
Grendon Ct. Teign —4C 8
Grenville Av. Teign —2C 8
Grenville Av. Torq —3G 19
Grenville Clo. Dart —4A 30
Grenville Clo. New A —2B 12
Grenville Way. Good —3E 25
Greycoat La. New A —4A 6
Greystone Way. Torq —2C 20
Groper's La. Comp —1A 18
Grosvenor Av. Torq —6B 16
Grosvenor Clo. Torq —6B 16
Grosvenor Rd. Paign —6E 23
Grosvenor Ter. Paign —6E 23
Grosvenor Ter. Teign —3D 8
Grove Av. Teign —4D 8

Grove Clo. *Tot* —4F **31**
Grove Ct. *Daw* —4F **3**
Grove Ct. *Teign* —3E **9**
Grove Cres. *Teign* —4D **8**
Grove Ter. *Teign* —4D **8**
Grove, The. *Paign* —2B **24**
Grove, The. *Tot* —4F **31**
Guestland Rd. *Torq* —2D **20**
Guildhall Yd. *Tot* —4F **31**
Gurneys, The. *Paign* —6D **22**

Haccombe Path. *New A* —3C **12**
Hackney La. *Kgstn* —5G **7**
(in two parts)
Hackney La. *Neth* —6H **7**
Hadfield Ct. *Chud* —1H **5**
Halcyon Rd. *New A* —2G **11**
Haldon Av. *Teign* —3E **9**
Haldon Clo. *New A* —3C **12**
Haldon Clo. *Torq* —5F **21**
Haldon Ri. *New A* —3C **12**
Haldon Rd. *Torq* —5E **21**
Haldon Ter. Daw —4D 2
(off Hospital Hill)
Hall La. *Holc* —1G **9**
Hall's La. *Kgswl* —3G **15**
Halsteads Rd. *Torq* —5F **17**
Hameldown Clo. *Torq* —2E **19**
Hameldown Way. *New A* —1A **12**
Hamelin Way. *Comp & Kgswl* —2C **18**
Hamilton Dri. *New A* —1G **11**
Hamiltons, The. *Shal* —6C **8**
Ham La. *Dit* —4A **26**
Ham La. *Shal* —6B **8**
Hamlyns Way. *Buckf* —4B **32**
Hampton Av. *Torq* —1D **20**
Hampton Clo. *Torq* —1D **20**
Hampton La. *Torq* —1D **20**
Hampton Rd. *New A* —2H **11**
Hanover Clo. *Brix* —4D **28**
Happaway Clo. *Torq* —5F **17**
Happaway Rd. *Torq* —5E **17**
Harberton Clo. *Paign* —2B **24**
Harbourne Av. *Paign* —2B **24**
Harbour Vw. Clo. *Brix* —2D **28**
Hardy Clo. *Torq* —6E **21**
Hares La. *Ashb* —4F **33**
Harper's Hill. *Tot* —4E **31**
(in two parts)
Harpins Ct. *Kgswl* —1H **15**
Hartland Tor Clo. *Brix* —5B **28**
Hartley Rd. *Paign* —6D **22**
Hartop Rd. *Torq* —6G **17**
Harts Clo. *Teign* —3C **8**
Haslam Ct. *Torq* —2B **20**
Haslam Rd. *Torq* —2B **20**
Hatchcombe La. *Torq* —5E **17**
Hatcher St. *Daw* —4D **2**
Hatfield Rd. *Torq* —3C **20**
Hauley Rd. *Dart* —4C **30** (2B **30**)
Havelock Rd. *Torq* —6G **17**
Haven, The. *Bish* —5G **9**
Hawkesway. *Tot* —4F **31**
Hawkins Av. *Torq* —2F **19**
Hawkins Dri. *Teign* —3D **8**
Hawkins Rd. *New A* —2C **12**
Hawthorn Clo. *New A* —5C **12**
Hawthorn Pk. Clo. *Torq* —6G **19**
Hawthorn Ri. *Torq* —4D **16**
Haycock La. *Brix* —2F **29**
Hayes Clo. *Tot* —5H **31**
Hayes Gdns. *Paign* —1D **24**
Hayes Rd. *Paign* —1C **24**
Hayes, The. *Chur F* —2H **27**
Hayle Av. *Paign* —5E **25**
Haytor Av. *Paign* —3C **24**
Haytor Clo. *Teign* —3B **8**
Haytor Dri. *New A* —2C **12**
Haytor Gro. *New A* —2D **12**
Haytor Ho. Cvn. Site. Kgstn —4F 7
(off Crossley Moor Rd.)
Haytor Rd. *Torq* —2C **20**
Haytor Rd. *Bov T* —3A **4**
Haytor Ter. *New A* —2G **11**
Haytor Vw. *Heath* —3F **5**
Haywain Clo. *Torq* —6A **16**
Hazel Av. *Torq* —1F **19**
Hazel Clo. *Teign* —1D **8**
Hazel Clo. *New A* —4D **12**
Hazeldown Rd. *Teign* —2D **8**
Headborough Rd. *Ashb* —3E **33**
Headland Gro. *Paign* —2F **23**
Headland Pk. Rd. *Paign* —2F **23**
Headland Rd. *Torq* —1H **23**
Headway Clo. *Teign* —4B **8**
Headway Cross Rd. *Teign* —3B **8**
Headway Ri. *Teign* —3B **8**
Heath Clo. *Heath* —4F **5**
Heath Ct. *Brix* —2F **29**
Heather Clo. *New A* —1E **11**
Heather Clo. *Teign* —2D **8**
Heatherdene. *Bov T* —3B **4**
Heather Est. *Heath* —3E **5**
Heather Way. *Brix* —3B **28**
Heathfield Bus. Pk. *Heath* —3E **5**
Heathfield Clo. *Bov T* —5B **4**
Heathfield Cotts. *Heath* —3F **5**
Heathfield Mdw. *Bov T* —5B **4**
Heathfield Ter. *Bov T* —4B **4**
Heath Hill. *Heath* —4F **5**
Heath Pk. *Brix* —2F **29**
Heath Pk. *New A* —4D **12**
Heath Ri. *Brix* —2F **29**
Heath Rd. *Brix* —2E **29**
Heath Way. *Tot* —4F **31**
Heatree Clo. *Teign* —1D **8**
Heaviside Clo. *Torq* —4G **17**
Hedgehog Hospital at Prickly Ball Farm. —6E 11
Hele Clo. *Torq* —6E **17**
Helens Mead Clo. *Torq* —3F **17**
Helens Mead Rd. *Torq* —3F **17**
Hele Rd. *Kgstn* —2E **7**
Hele Rd. *Torq* —6D **16**
Helford Dri. *Paign* —5E **25**
Helford Wlk. *Paign* —5E **25**
Heligan Dri. *Paign* —3B **22**
Hellevoetsluis Way. *Marl* —6B **18**
Helmdon Ri. *Torq* —1E **19**
Helston Clo. *Paign* —4C **22**
Hembury Cock Hill. *Buck* —2A **32**
Hembury Pk. *Buck* —2B **32**
Hems Brook Ct. *Torq* —1E **19**
Henbury Clo. *Torq* —3C **20**
Hennapyn Rd. *Torq* —6H **19**
Hennock Rd. *Paign* —3C **24**
Hensford Rd. *Daw* —1C **2**
Henty Av. *Daw* —3F **3**
Henty Clo. *Daw* —2F **3**
Herbert Rd. *Torq* —5G **19**
Hermitage Rd. *Dart* —3A **30**
Hermosa Gdns. *Teign* —4D **8**
Hermosa Rd. *Teign* —4D **8**
Heron Way. *Torq* —4B **16**
Hesketh Cres. *Torq* —6E **21**
Hesketh Rd. *Torq* —6E **21**
Hestow Rd. *Kgstn* —1F **7**
Hewett Clo. *New A* —2D **12**
Heywood Clo. *Torq* —2G **19**
Heywoods Clo. Teign —4E 9
(off Heywoods Rd.)
Heywoods Rd. *Teign* —4E **9**
Highbury Rd. *Torq* —3C **20**
Highcliffe M. *Paign* —1F **25**
High Clo. *Bov T* —3D **4**
Higher Audley Av. *Torq* —1A **20**
Higher Bibbery. *Bov T* —3D **4**
Higher Brimley. *Teign* —3D **8**
Higher Brimley Rd. *Teign* —4D **8**
Higher Broad Pk. *Dart* —4A **30**
Higher Brook St. *Teign* —4D **8**
Higher Buckeridge Rd. *Teign* —2D **8**
Higher Budleigh Mdw. *New A* —2E **11**
Higher Cadewell La. *Torq* —6A **16**
Higher Coombe Dri. *Teign* —2C **8**
Higher Copythorne. *Brix* —3B **28**
Higher Downs Rd. *Torq* —1D **20**
Higher Dri. *Daw* —2F **3**
Higher Edginswell La. *Torq* —2D **18**
Higher Erith Rd. *Torq* —5E **21**
Higher Exeter Rd. *Teign* —1C **8**
Higher French Pk. *New A* —2E **11**
Higher Furzeham Rd. *Brix* —1D **28**
Higher Holcombe Clo. *Teign* —2E **9**
Higher Holcombe Dri. *Teign* —1E **9**
Higher Holcombe Rd. *Teign* —1E **9**
Higher Kingsdown Rd. *Teign* —4B **8**
Higher Lincombe Rd. *Torq* —6E **21**
Higher Mnr. Rd. *Brix* —2D **28**
Higher Mnr. Ter. Paign —6D 22
(off Manor Ter.)
Higher Mill La. *Buck* —2B **32**
(in two parts)
Higher Penn. *Brix* —4E **29**
Higher Polsham Rd. *Paign* —4E **23**
Higher Queen's Ter. *Torq* —4C **20**
Higher Ramshill La. *Paign* —3A **22**
Higher Ranscombe Rd. *Brix* —3E **29**
Higher Ringmore Rd. *Shal* —6A **8**
Higher Roborough. *Ashb* —3G **33**
Higher Rydons. *Brix* —3B **28**
Higher Sackery. *Combe* —1G **13**
Higher Sandygate. *Kgstn* —1E **7**
Higher St. *Brix* —2D **28**
Higher St. *Dart* —4C **30** (1B **30**)
Higher St. *Kgswr* —5D **30**
Higher Union La. *Torq* —4B **20**
Higher Warberry Rd. *Torq* —4D **20**
Higher Warborough Rd. *Galm* —1E **27**
Higher Westonfields. *Tot* —4H **31**
Higher Woodfield Rd. *Torq* —6D **20**
Higher Woodway Clo. *Teign* —2E **9**
Higher Woodway Rd. *Teign* —1D **8**
Higher Yannon Dri. *Teign* —3C **8**
Highfield Clo. *Brix* —3B **28**
Highfield Cres. *Paign* —5B **22**
Highgrove Pk. *Teign* —2E **9**
High Ho. Clo. *Daw* —3E **3**
Highland Clo. *Torq* —3F **19**
Highland Rd. *Torq* —3F **19**
High St. *Daw* —4D **2**
High St. *Tot* —4E **31**
Highweek Clo. *New A* —6A **6**
Highweek Rd. *New A* —1F **11**
(in two parts)
Highweek Village. *New A* —6A **6**
Highweek Way. *New A* —2G **11**
Highwood Clo. *New A* —3G **11**
Hillbrook Ri. *Tot* —4H **31**
Hillbrook Rd. *Tot* —4H **31**
Hilldown. *Tot* —4H **31**
Hilldrop Ter. *Torq* —4C **20**
Hiller La. *New A* —3E **13**
Hillesdon Rd. *Torq* —4C **20**
Hillfield. *Sto G* —6A **24**
Hillmans Rd. *New A* —3H **11**
Hill Pk. Clo. *Brix* —3F **29**
Hill Pk. Rd. *Brix* —3F **29**
Hill Pk. Rd. *New A* —1E **11**
Hill Pk. Rd. *Torq* —2B **20**
Hill Pk. Ter. *Paign* —6F **23**
Hillrise. *Galm* —2E **27**
Hill Rd. *New A* —3G **11**
Hillside Camp. *Good* —4E **25**
Hillside Clo. *Teign* —2B **8**
Hillside Cotts. *Abbot* —1B **14**
Hillside Ct. *Dart* —4B **30**
Hillside Rd. *Brix* —3D **28**
Hillside Rd. *Paign* —4C **22**
Hillside Ter. Paign —5D 22
(off Colley End Pk.)
Hill Vw. *Holc* —1G **9**
Hill Vw. Ter. *Torq* —2B **20**
Hilly Gdns. Rd. *Torq* —6G **17**
Hilton Cres. *Pres* —1F **23**
Hilton Dri. *Pres* —2F **23**
Hilton Rd. *New A* —3H **11**
Hind St. *Bov T* —2C **4**
Hingston Rd. *Torq* —2D **20**
Hodson Clo. *Paign* —4C **22**
Hoile La. *Sto G* —5A **24**
Holbeam Clo. *New A* —1D **10**
Holbeam La. *New A* —1A **10**
Holborn Rd. *Brix* —1D **28**
Holcombe Down Rd. *Teign & Daw* (in two parts) —1D **8**
Holcombe Dri. *Daw* —1H **9**
Holcombe Rd. *Holc* —6C **2**
Holcombe Rd. *Teign & Daw* —2G **9**
Holcombe Village. *Holc* —1G **9**
Hollacombe La. *Paign* —2G **23**
Hollam Way. *Kgstn* —3G **7**
Hollands Rd. *Teign* —5E **9**
Hollywater Clo. *Torq* —4E **21**
Holman Clo. *Daw* —2F **3**
Holmes Ct. *Tot* —3F **31**
Holmes Rd. *Heath* —4E **5**
Holne Moor Clo. *Paign* —4B **22**
Holne Rd. *Buckf* —2A **32**
Holwell Rd. *Brix* —3C **28**
Holwill Tor Wlk. *Paign* —2C **24**
Home Clo. *Brix* —4D **28**
Homefield Cotts. *Torq* —2E **21**
Home Mdw. *Tot* —4F **31**
Home Pk. *Ashb* —3F **33**
Homers Clo. *Kgstn* —5E **7**
Homers Cres. *Kgstn* —5E **7**
Homers La. *Kgstn* —5E **7**
Homestead Rd. *Torq* —1B **20**
Homestead Ter. *Torq* —1B **20**
Hometeign Ho. New A —1A 12
(off Salisbury Rd.)
Homeyards Botanical Gardens, The. —6D 8
Homeyards, The. Shal —6C 8
(off Commons Old Rd.)
Honey La. *Dac* —1E **17**
Honeysuckle Clo. *Paign* —3B **22**
Honeywell. *Kgstn* —5F **7**
Honeywell Rd. *Kgstn* —5F **7**
Hoodown La. *Dart* —3D **30**
Hookhills Dri. *Paign* —4F **25**
Hookhills Gdns. *Paign* —5E **25**
Hookhills Gro. *Paign* —4F **25**
Hookhills Rd. *Paign* —5E **25**
Hook La. *Galm* —4D **26**
Hoopern Ter. Daw —4D 2
(off Penfield Gdns.)
Hope Clo. *Tot* —4H **31**
Hope's Clo. *Teign* —3C **8**
Hope Wlk. *Tot* —4H **31**

Hopkins La. *New A* —2H **11**
Horace Rd. *Torq* —5E **17**
Horn Hill Steps. *Dart —2A **30***
Horns Pk. *Bish* —5F **9**
Horse La. *Shal* —6D **8**
Horsepool St. *Brix* —4C **28**
Horseshoe Bend. *Paign* —3F **25**
Hosegood Way. *Kgstn* —4E **7**
Hoskings Ct. *Buckf* —4B **32**
Hospital Hill. *Daw* —4D **2**
Hospital La. *Ashb* —3H **33**
Hound Tor Clo. *Paign* —6E **25**
House of Marbles & Teign Valley Glass. —5B 4 (off Pottery Road)
Howard Clo. *Daw* —4D **2**
Howard Clo. *Teign* —2C **8**
Howard Clo. *Torq* —3G **19**
Howard Ct. *Teign* —2C **8**
Howards Way. *New A* —1C **12**
Howton Rd. *New A* —6A **6**
Hoxton Rd. *Torq* —4C **20**
Hoyle's Rd. *Paign* —3B **22**
Huccaby Clo. *Brix* —5A **28**
Humber La. *Kgstn* —3G **7**
Hunsdon Rd. *Torq* —5D **20**
Huntacott Way. *Torq* —1E **19**
Hunters Tor Dri. *Paign* —6E **25**
Hunterswell Rd. *New A* —2F **11**
Hutchings Way. *Teign* —3B **8**
Hutton Rd. *Paign* —2D **22**
Huxley Va. *Kgswl* —4G **15**
Huxnor Rd. *Kgswl* —4G **15**
Huxtable Hill. *Torq* —5G **19**
Hyde Rd. *Paign* —5E **23**

Iddesleigh Ter. *Daw* —4E **3**
Idewell Rd. *Torq* —5G **17**
Ilford Pk. *Stov* —6E **5**
Ilsham Clo. *Torq* —4G **21**
Ilsham Cres. *Torq* —5G **21**
Ilsham Marine Dri. *Torq* —6G **21**
Ilsham M. *Torq* —4F **21**
Ilsham Rd. *Torq* —4F **21**
Indio Rd. *Bov T* —4B **4**
Innerbrook Rd. *Torq* —4H **19**
Inverteign Dri. *Teign* —4B **8**
Ipplepen Rd. *Marl* —5A **18**
Isaacs Rd. *Torq* —4E **17**
Isambard Ct. *Torq* —4G **17**
Ivatt Rd. *Dart* —4A **30**
Ivy La. *Dart* —1A **30**
Ivy La. *Teign* —5D **8**

Jack's La. *Torq* —4E **17**
Jacolind Wlk. *Brix* —3E **29**
James Av. *Paign* —2B **22**
Jasmine Gro. *Paign* —3B **22**
Jawbones Hill. *Dart* —4C **30** (2A **30**)
Jellicoe Vs. *Tot* —4E **31**
Jetty Marsh Nature Reserve. —6D 6
Jetty Marsh Rd. *New A* —6C **6**
John Acres La. *Kgstn* —1C **6**
John Nash Dri. *Daw* —5C **2**
John's Av. *Torq* —1A **20**
Jonida Clo. *Torq* —2B **20**
Jordan Dri. *Teign* —3B **8**
Jordan Mdw. *Ashb* —3G **33**
Jordan St. *Buckf* —4A **32**
Joslin Ct. *Kgstn* —3E **7**
Jubilee Clo. *Dart* —4A **30**
Jubilee Clo. *Torq* —4C **20**
Jubilee Rd. *New A* —2G **11**
Jubilee Rd. *Tot* —3H **31**
Jubilee Ter. *Paign* —5D **22**
Jungle Express. —1C 24
Jurys Corner Clo. *Kgswl* —3H **15**

Keatings La. *Teign* —4C **8**
Keats Clo. *Teign* —2B **8**
Keep Gdns., The. *Dart* —4B **30**
Keep La. *Dart* —3B **30** (1A **30**)
Kelland Clo. *Paign* —5C **22**
Kellock Dri. *Tot* —4E **31**
Kelly Clo. *Torq* —6D **20**
Kelvin Ct. *Torq* —6H **17**
Kemmings Clo. *Paign* —4B **24** (in two parts)
Kendlewood Clo. *Paign* —2C **24**
Kennels Rd. *Chur F* —4F **27**
Kenneth Ct. *Torq* —1F **19**
Kensey Clo. *Torq* —3F **21**
Kenton Brook Ct. *Torq* —1E **19**
Kent's Cavern. —4F 21
Kent's La. *Torq* —4F **21**
Kent's Rd. *Torq* —4F **21**
Kenwyn Rd. *Torq* —3D **20**
Kernou Rd. *Paign* —5F **23**
Kerria Clo. *Paign* —3B **22**
Kerswell La. *Cof* —2H **15**
Kestor Dri. *Paign* —1D **22**
Keyberry Clo. *New A* —4A **12**
Keyberry Mill. *New A* —4A **12**
Keyberry Pk. *New A* —4A **12**
Keyberry Rd. *New A* —4A **12**
Keysfield Rd. *Paign* —6F **23**
Killerton Clo. *Paign* —4E **23**
Kilmorie. *Torq* —6G **21**
Kilmorie Clo. *Torq* —6G **21**
Kiln Clo. *Bov T* —5B **4**
Kilnford Rd. *Kgstn* —4G **7**
Kiln Forehead La. *Kgstn* —4G **7**
Kiln Orchard. *New A* —2E **11**
Kiln Path. *Brix* —3D **28**
Kiln Rd. *Galm* —3D **26**
Kiln Rd. *Bov T* —5B **4**
Kiln Rd. *Marl* —6A **18**
*Kimberley Cotts. Teign —5E **9** (off Bickford La.)*
King Charles I Bus. Pk. *Heath* —2E **5**
Kingcome Ct. *Buckf* —4C **32**
Kingfisher Clo. *Torq* —5C **16**
King's Ash Rd. *Paign* —2B **22**
Kings Av. *Paign* —4F **23**
Kingsbridge Hill. *Tot* —5F **31**
Kingsbridge La. *Ashb* —4F **33**
Kings Coombe Dri. *Kgstn* —2F **7**
Kings Cotts. *New A* —2H **11**
Kings Ct. *Kgstn* —5F **7**
Kings Ct. *Kgswl* —3G **15**
Kingsdale Ct. *Torq* —5C **20**
Kingsdown Clo. *Daw* —3E **3**
Kingsdown Clo. *Teign* —4B **8**
Kingsdown Cres. *Daw* —3E **3**
Kingsdown Rd. *Teign* —4B **8**
King's Dri., The. *Torq* —5A **20**
Kingsgate Clo. *Torq* —3G **17**
Kingshurst Dri. *Paign* —3E **23**
Kingskerswell Rd. *Kgswl & Torq* —6B **16**
Kingskerswell Rd. *New A* —4A **12**
Kingsland Dri. *Paign* —1B **24**
Kings Mdw. *Kgstn* —3G **15**
Kings Orchard. *Tot* —4H **31**
*Kings Quay. Dart —3C **30** (off Mayors Av.)*
Kings Rd. *Paign* —4F **23**
Kings Rydon Clo. *Sto G* —5A **24**
Kingsteignton Ind. Est. *Kgstn* —5E **7**
Kingsteignton Rd. *New A* —1H **11**
Kingston Clo. *Kgswl* —2H **15**
Kingston La. *Dart* —4A **30**
King St. *Brix* —2E **29**
King St. *Daw* —4D **2**
King St. *New A* —2H **11**
King's Wlk. *Daw* —5E **3**
Kingswater Ct. *Brix* —2D **28**
Kingsway. *Teign* —4B **8**
Kingsway Av. *Paign* —4D **24**
Kingsway Clo. *Paign* —4D **24**
Kingsway Ct. *Paign* —4D **24**
Kingsway Dri. *Paign* —4D **24**
Kingswear Rd. *Brix* —6H **27**
Kintyre Clo. *Torq* —5D **16**
Kirkham House. —5E 23 (off Kirkham Street)
Kirkham St. *Paign* —4E **23**
Kirkstead Clo. *Torq* —1H **19**
*Kistor Gdns. Tot —3F **31** (off Castle St.)*
Knapp Pk. Rd. *Paign* —3F **25**
Knebworth Ct. *Torq* —6H **17**
Knick Knack La. *Brix* —4D **28**
Knowles Hill Rd. *New A* —1G **11**

Laburnum Ct. *Abbot* —1C **14**
Laburnum Rd. *New A* —4B **12**
Laburnum Row. *Torq* —3A **20**
Laburnum St. *Torq* —4A **20**
Laburnum Ter. *Abbot* —6G **11**
Lacy Rd. *Paign* —2D **22**
Ladies Mile. *Daw* —3G **3**
Lady Pk. Rd. *Torq* —6G **19**
Lady's Mile Touring & Cvn. Pk. *Daw* —1F **3**
Lake Av. *Teign* —2C **8**
Lakeland. *Abbot* —1C **14**
Lakes Clo. *Brix* —2B **28**
Lakeside Clo. *Bov T* —6B **4**
Lakes Rd. *Brix* —3B **28**
Lake St. *Dart* —4C **30** (1A **30**)
Lamacraft Clo. *Daw* —2F **3**
Lambert Clo. *Daw* —2F **3**
Lamb Pk. Clo. *Kgstn* —1F **7**
Lamb, The. *Tot* —4E **31**
Lammas La. *Paign & Pres* —3C **22**
Lancaster Dri. *Paign* —3C **24**
Landscore Clo. *Teign* —4D **8**
Landscore Rd. *Teign* —4C **8**
Landscove Holiday Village. *Brix* —3G **29**
Lands Rd. *Brix* —1F **29**
Lane, The. *Dit* —5A **26**
Langaller Clo. *Bov T* —5A **4**
Langaller La. *Bov T* —6A **4**
Langdon Fields. *Galm* —1E **27**
Langdon La. *Daw* —1C **2**
Langdon La. *Galm* —2E **27**
Langdon Rd. *Daw* —1C **2**
Langdon Rd. *Paign* —2F **23**
Langford Cres. *Torq* —4E **17**
Langlands Clo. *Paign* —1B **24**
Langley Av. *Brix* —3D **28**
Langley Clo. *Brix* —3D **28**
Langridge Rd. *Paign* —3B **22**
Langs Rd. *Paign* —3F **23**
Langstone Clo. *Heath* —4E **5**
Langstone Clo. *Torq* —2E **21**
Lang Way. *Ippn* —5C **14**
Lanherne. *Daw* —4E **3**
Lanhydrock Clo. *Paign* —3A **22**
Lansdowne La. *Torq* —3A **20**
Lansdowne Pk. *Tot* —5H **31**
Lansdowne Rd. *Torq* —4A **20**
Larch Clo. *Teign* —1D **8**
Larch Wlk. *Torq* —1F **19**
Larks Clo. *Shal* —6B **8**
Larksmead Clo. *Ogwl* —4F **11**
Larksmead Way. *Ogwl* —4E **11**
Laura Av. *Paign* —3E **23**
Laura Gro. *Paign & Pres* —3C **22**
Laurel La. *Shal* —6B **8**
Laureston Rd. *New A* —3H **11**
Laurie Av. *New A* —1E **11**
Lauriston Clo. *Torq* —4A **20**
Lavender Clo. *Brix* —3B **28**
Lawn Clo. *Torq* —4E **17**
Lawn Hill. *Daw* —4E **3**
Lawns End. *Bish* —5F **9**
Lawn Ter. *Daw* —4E **3**
*Lawrence Pl. Torq —5C **20** (off Strand)*
Laywell Clo. *Brix* —5C **28**
Laywell Rd. *Brix* —4B **28**
Lea Cliff Pk. *Daw W* —1H **3**
Leader La. *Marl* —1A **22**
Lealands. *Bov T* —4B **4**
Lea Mt. *Bish* —5H **9**
Lea Mt. Clo. *Daw* —5D **2**
Lea Mt. Dri. *Daw* —5D **2**
Lea Mt. Rd. *Daw* —5E **3**
Lea Rd. *Torq* —4G **17**
Lea, The. *Teign* —5H **9** (in two parts)
Leat Ter. *Kgstn* —4F **7**
Lea Va. Rd. *New A* —2F **11**
Leaze Rd. *Kgstn* —3E **7**
Ledsgrove. *Ippn* —5C **14**
Leechwell La. *Tot* —4F **31** (in two parts)
Leechwell St. *Tot* —4F **31** (in two parts)
Lee Ct. *Brix* —3F **29**
Leigham Ct. *Daw* —4E **3**
Leighon Rd. *Paign* —5F **23**
Le Molay-Littry Way. *Bov T* —3C **4**
Lemon Pl. *New A* —2H **11**
Lemon Rd. *New A* —2H **11**
Leyburn Gro. *Paign* —1D **24**
*Leyfield Wlk. Daw —3E **3** (off Gatehouse Hill)*
Ley La. *Kgstn* —3E **7**
Leys Rd. *Torq* —4G **19**
Lichfield Av. *Torq* —5F **17**
Lichfield Clo. *Brix* —3B **28**
Lichfield Dri. *Brix* —3B **28**
Lidford Tor Av. *Paign* —2B **24**
Light La. *Galm* —3E **27**
Lime Av. *Torq* —4A **20**
Lime Tree Wlk. *New A* —4B **12**
Linacre La. *Cof* —1B **16**
Linacre Rd. *Torq* —4E **17**
Lincoln Grn. *Torq* —6F **17**
Lincombe Dri. *Torq* —6E **21**
Lincombe Hill Rd. *Torq* —5F **21**
Linden Rd. *Daw* —5C **2**
Linden Ter. *New A* —2F **11**
Lindisfarne Way. *Torq* —5D **16**
Lindridge Clo. *Kgstn* —1E **7**
Lindridge Hill. *Kgstn* —1F **7**
Lindridge La. *Kgstn* —1E **7**
Lindridge Rd. *Torq* —1D **20**
Lindsay Rd. *Pres* —1D **22**
Lindthorpe Way. *Brix* —3C **28**
Linhay Bus. Pk. *Ashb* —2H **33**
Links Clo. *Chur F* —1H **27**
Lisburne Cres. *Torq* —5E **21**
Lisburne Sq. *Torq* —5E **21**
Lit. Barton. *Kgstn* —2F **7**
Lit. Bossell La. *Buckf* —5B **32**
Little Clo. *Kgstn* —2F **7**
Littlefield. *Bish* —5F **9**
Littlefield Clo. *Torq* —6C **16**
Littlegate Rd. *Paign* —5E **23**
Lit. Hayes. *Kgstn* —2F **7**
Littlejoy Rd. *New A* —2A **10**

Lit. Park Rd. Paign —5D 22
Lit. Roborough. Ashb —3F 33
Lit. Triangle. Teign —5E 9 (off Triangle Pl.)
Lit. Week Clo. Daw —1F 3
Lit. Week La. Daw —1F 3
Lit. Week Rd. Daw —1F 3
Livermead Hill. Torq —1H 23
Livingstone Rd. Teign —3E 9
Lloyd Av. Torq —1G 19
Locarno Av. Paign —2G 23
Locks Clo. Torq —2E 21
Locks Hill. Torq —2E 21
Locksley Clo. Torq —2C 20
Logan Rd. Paign —4F 23
Long Barton. Kgstn —2F 7
Longcroft Av. Brix —4C 28
Longcroft Dri. Brix —4C 28
Longfield Av. Kgstn —4G 7
Longford La. Kgstn —3F 7
Longford Pk. Kgstn —3F 7
Longlands. Daw —4D 2
Long La. Daw —1B 2
Long La. Hacc —4E 13
Long La. Shal —6A 8
Longmead Rd. Paign —2C 22
Longmead Wlk. Paign —2C 22
Long Pk. Ashb & Chag —2G 33
Long Pk. Hill. Maid —1H 17
Long Rd. Paign —3A 24
Long Rydon. Sto G —5A 24
Longstone Rd. Paign —1B 24
Long Wools. Paign —6G 25
Lonsdale Rd. New A —3A 12
Lord's Pl. Torq —3C 20
Lorris Dri. Teign —3C 8
Louville Camp. Brix —2G 29
Louville Clo. Paign —3F 25
Love La. Teign —2F 9
Love La. Marl —5A 18
Love La. Clo. Marl —5A 18
Lwr. Audley Rd. Torq —1A 20
Lwr. Blagdon La. Paign —5A 22
Lwr. Brimley. Teign —3E 9
Lwr. Brimley Clo. Teign —4E 9
Lwr. Broad Pk. Dart —4A 30
Lwr. Broad Path. Sto G —6B 24
Lwr. Brook St. Teign —5E 9
Lwr. Budleigh Mdw. New A —2E 11
Lwr. Cannon Rd. Heath —4E 5
Lwr. Collapark. Tot —3E 31
Lwr. Collins Rd. Tot —3E 31
Lwr. Congella Rd. Torq —3D 20
Lwr. Contour Rd. Kgswr —4D 30
Lwr. Coombe Rd. Kgstn —4G 7
Lwr. Dawlish Water. Daw —2A 2
Lower Dri. Daw —2F 3
Lwr. Ellacombe Chu. Rd. Torq —3D 20
Lwr. Erith Rd. Torq —5E 21
Lwr. Fairview Rd. Dart —4B 30
Lwr. Fern Rd. New A —5C 12
Lwr. Fowden. Paign —1G 27
Lwr. French Pk. New A —2E 11
Lwr. Kingsdown Rd. Teign —4B 8
Lwr. Manor Rd. Brix —2D 28
Lower Mdw. Ri. Daw —4C 2
Lwr. Penns Rd. Pres —2F 23
Lwr. Polsham Rd. Paign —4E 23
Lwr. Rea Rd. Brix —2E 29
Lwr. Sandygate. Kgstn —1E 7
Lwr. Shirburn Rd. Torq —2B 20
Lower St. Dart & Dit —4C 30 (2B 30)
Lwr. Thurlow Rd. Torq —3B 20
Lwr. Union La. Torq —4B 20
Lwr. Warberry Rd. Torq —4C 20
Lwr. Woodfield Rd. Torq —6D 20
Lwr. Yalberton Rd. Paign —3A 24
Lowley Brook Ct. Torq —1E 19
Loxbury Ri. Torq —5G 19
Loxbury Rd. Torq —4G 19
Lucerne. Torq —5E 21
Lucius St. Torq —4A 20
Lulworth Clo. Paign —3C 24
Lummaton Cross. Torq —5F 17
Lummaton Pl. Torq —6G 17
Luscombe Clo. Ippn —6B 14
Luscombe Cres. Paign —5B 22
Luscombe Hill. Daw —4A 2
Luscombe M. Tot —4G 31 (off Bridgetown)
Luscombe Rd. Paign —3A 22
Luscombe Ter. Daw —4D 2
Lutyens Dri. Paign —4A 22
Luxton Rd. Ogwl —5E 11
Lydwell Pk. Rd. Torq —3E 21
Lydwell Rd. Torq —3E 21
Lyme Bay Rd. Teign —2E 9
Lyme Vw. Clo. Torq —2E 21
Lyme Vw. Rd. Torq —2D 20
Lymington Rd. Torq —2A 20
Lyncombe Cres. Torq —6F 21
Lyndale Rd. Kgstn —3E 7
Lyndhurst Av. Kgswl —2H 15
Lyndhurst Clo. Kgswl —2H 15
Lyn Gro. Kgswl —1G 15
Lynmouth Av. Paign —3C 24
Lynwood. Ogwl —4E 11
Lyte's Rd. Brix —3E 29

Mabel Pl. Paign —6E 23
Mackrells Ter. New A —3F 11
Maddacombe Rd. Kgswl —3E 15
Maddicks Orchard. Sto G —6A 24
Madrepore Pl. Torq —4C 20 (off Madrepore Rd.)
Madrepore Rd. Torq —5C 20
Magdalene Clo. Tot —4F 31
Magdalene Rd. Torq —3A 20
Maidenway La. Paign —3C 22
Maidenway Rd. Paign —3C 22
Main Av. Torq —1B 20
Malderek Av. Paign —2F 23
Mallands Mdw. New A —6F 11
Mallock Rd. Torq —4H 19
Malt Mill La. Tot —3E 31
Manaton Tor Rd. Paign —2C 22
Mannings Mdw. Bov T —3C 4
Manor Av. Paign —3F 23
Manor Bend. Galm —2F 27
Manor Clo. Abbot —6F 11
Manor Clo. Daw —4D 2
Manor Clo. Kgswl —4H 15
Manor Cotts. New A —2G 11 (off Gothic Rd.)
Manor Cres. Paign —3F 23
Manor Dri. Kgswl —4H 15
Manor Gdns. Kgswl —4H 15
Manor Gdns. Paign —3F 23
Manor Gdns. Torq —6F 21
Manor Gdns. Abbot —1C 14
Manor Rd. Abbot —6F 11
Manor Rd. Bish —5G 9
Manor Rd. New A —2E 11
Manor Rd. Paign —3F 23
Manor Rd. Torq —1C 20
Manor Steps. Brix —2D 28
Manor St. Dit —5A 26
Manor Ter. Brix —2D 28
Manor Ter. Paign —6D 22
Manor Va. Rd. Galm —2F 27
Manor Vw. New A —2F 11
Manor Way. Tot —4F 31
Mansbridge Rd. Tot —4H 31
Manscombe Clo. Torq —6G 19
Manscombe Rd. Torq —1G 23
Mansion Ho. St. Dart —2B 30
Maple Clo. Brix —5B 28
Maple Clo. Kgstn —5F 7
Maple Clo. Chud —1H 5
Mapledene Clo. Sto G —5A 24
Maple Rd. Brix —5B 28 (in two parts)
Mapleton Clo. New A —1E 11
Maple Wlk. Torq —1F 19
Marcombe Rd. Torq —4H 19
Mardle Way. Buckf —4B 32
Margaret Clo. Ogwl —4E 11
Margaret Clo. Kgstn —4F 7
Margaret Gdns. New A —3C 12
Margaret Rd. Kgstn —4F 7
Margaret Rd. Ogwl —4E 11
Marguerite Clo. New A —1E 11
Marguerite Way. Kgswl —3H 15
Marina Clo. Brix —2F 29
Marina Dri. Brix —2F 29
Marina Rd. Brix —3F 29
Marine Dri. Paign —4F 23
Marine Gdns. Paign —3F 23
Marine Pde. Daw —5E 3
Marine Pde. Paign —3G 23
Marine Pde. Shal —6D 8
Marine Pk. Paign —4F 23
Marine Pk. Holiday Cen. Good —3E 25
Mariners Way. Paign —2C 22
Marine Ter. Teign —5D 8 (off Foresters Ter.)
Market Clo. Buckf —4A 32
Market Sq. Dart —4C 30 (1A 30)
Market Sq. New A —2G 11
Market St. Brix —2D 28
Market St. Dart —4C 30 (1A 30)
Market St. New A —2G 11
Market St. Torq —4C 20
Market St. Buckf —4B 32
Market Wlk. New A —2G 11
Marlborough Av. Torq —4E 21
Marlborough Pl. New A —1F 11
Marlborough Ter. Bov T —3A 4
Marldon Av. Paign —5D 22
Marldon Cross Hill. Marl —6A 18
Marldon Gro. Marl —6A 18
Marldon Rd. Paign —2B 22
Marldon Rd. Torq —3C 18
Marldon Way. Marl —1B 22
Marlowe Clo. Torq —2G 19
Marnham Rd. Torq —2C 20
Marsh Path. Bov T —3B 4
Marsh Rd. New A —2H 11
Marston Clo. Daw —3F 3
Mary St. Bov T —2B 4
Mashford Av. Dart —3A 30
Mathill Clo. Brix —4C 28
Mathill Rd. Brix —4C 28
Maudlin Dri. Teign —1D 8
Maudlin Rd. Tot —4F 31
Mayfair Rd. Ippn —5B 14
Mayfield Cres. New A —2E 11
Mayflower Av. New A —3C 12
Mayflower Clo. Dart —3A 30
Mayflower Clo. Daw —4E 3
Mayflower Dri. Brix —4D 28
Mayor's Av. Dart —4C 30 (1B 30)
Mead Clo. Paign —4E 23
Meadfoot Clo. Torq —5G 21
Meadfoot Ct. Torq —6D 20
Meadfoot La. Torq —6D 20
Meadfoot Rd. Torq —6D 20
Meadfoot Sea Rd. Torq —6E 21
Mead La. Paign —4E 23
Meadow Clo. Kgswl —1G 15
Meadow Clo. Hbtn & Tot —4H 31
Meadowcroft Dri. Kgstn —2E 7
Meadow Halt. Ogwl —3F 11
Meadow Pk. Brix —2C 28
Meadow Pk. Daw —3C 2
Meadow Pk. Ippn —5C 14
Meadow Pk. Teign —2B 8
Meadow Pk. Marl —6A 18
Meadow Ri. Daw —3C 2
Meadow Ri. Teign —2B 8
Meadow Rd. Torq —6H 19
Meadowside Holiday Cen. Good —4E 25
Meadows, The. Kgstn —5G 7
Meadow Vw. Ogwl —4E 11
Mead Rd. Torq —1G 23
Mead Way. Dec I —5A 12
Meavy Av. Torq —2E 19
Medway Rd. Torq —5G 17
Melbourne Cotts. Dart —2A 30
Melcot Clo. Kgstn —4F 7
Meldrum Clo. Daw —4E 3
Mellons Clo. New A —1C 10
Mellons Wlk. New A —1C 10 (off Mellons Clo.)
Mellows Mdw. New A —2E 11
Melville La. Torq —5C 20
Melville St. Torq —5C 20
Mena Pk. Clo. Paign —3C 24
Mendip Rd. Torq —6F 19
Mere La. Teign —4E 9
Merivale Clo. Teign —2E 9
Merlin Way. Torq —5C 16
Merrifield Rd. Buckf —3A 32
Merritt Flats. Paign —6D 22 (off Totnes Rd.)
Merritt Flats. Paign —6D 22 (off Merritt Rd.)
Merritt Rd. Paign —6D 22
Merrivale Clo. Torq —3G 17
Merrylands Clo. Paign —1E 23
Merrylands Gdns. Paign —1E 23
Merrywood. Ogwl —4E 11
Metherell Av. Brix —4D 28
Mews, The. Daw —4E 3
Meyrick Rd. Torq —2D 20
Middle Budleigh Mdw. New A —2E 11
Middle Lincombe Rd. Torq —6E 21
Middle St. Brix —2D 28
Middle St. Shal —6C 8
Middle Warberry Rd. Torq —4D 20
Midvale Rd. Paign —6E 23
Midway. Kgswl —1G 15
Milber La. New A —3D 12
Milber Trad. Est. New A —4D 12
Mile End Rd. New A —1D 10
Milford Clo. Teign —4C 8
Millbrook Pk. Rd. Torq —4H 19
Millbrook Rd. Paign —5E 23
Millbrook Vs. Torq —4H 19 (off Old Mill Rd.)
Mill Clo. New A —1D 10
Mill Ct. Daw —4C 2
Mill Cres. Dart —3A 30
Mill End. Kgstn —1F 7
Mill Hill. Sto G —6A 24
Mill Hill Ct. Sto G —6A 24
Mill La. Brix —6B 28
Mill La. Galm —3C 26
Mill La. Ogwl —4C 10
Mill La. Paign —4E 23
Mill La. Teign —3B 8
Mill La. Torq —4A 20
Mill La. Tot —4G 31
Mill La. Whil —5D 14 (in two parts)
Mill La. Ashb —3E 33

Mill Leat. New A —2A 10
Millmans Rd. Marl —6A 18
Mill Mdw. Ashb —3E 33
Mill Tail. Tot —4F 31
Milton Clo. Brix —5C 28
Milton Cres. Brix —5C 28
Milton Fields. Brix —5B 28
Milton Ho. New A —3H 11
Milton La. Dart —5A 30
Milton Pk. Brix —5C 28
Milton Rd. New A —1G 11
Milton St. Brix —6B 28
Minacre La. Kgswl —6F 15
Mincent Clo. Torq —4F 17
Mincent Hill. Torq —4F 17
Minden Rd. Teign —4D 8
Minerva Bus. Pk. New A —2A 12
Minerva Way. New A —2A 12
Miranda Rd. Pres —3C 22
Moat Hill. Tot —5F 31
Moles La. Marl —2C 18
Monastery Rd. Paign —5D 22
Monksbridge Rd. Brix —4C 28
Monks Orchard. Abbot —1B 14
Monks Way. Bov T —1A 4
(in two parts)
Monterey Clo. Torq —6H 19
Montpelier Ct. Paign —2E 23
Montpellier Rd. Torq —5C 20
Montpellier Ter. Torq —5C 20
(off Montpellier Rd.)
Moorashes. Tot —4F 31
(off St Katherine's Way)
Moor Clo. Teign —2E 9
Moore Clo. New A —5C 12
Moorhayes. Bov T —3C 4
Moorings Reach. Brix —2E 29
Moorland Av. Den —6A 10
Moorland Ga. Heath —4F 5
Moorlands Clo. New A —3C 12
Moorland Vw. New A —3C 12
Moorland Vw. Buckf —4A 32
Moor La. Torq —4F 17
Moor La. Bov T —5B 4
Moor La. Clo. Torq —4F 17
Moor Pk. Kgswl —1G 15
Moor Pk. Rd. Kgswl —1G 15
Moor Rd. Ippn —4A 14
Moors End. Brad V & Kgstn —4E 7
Moorsend. Brad V & Kgstn —1D 10
Moors Pk. Bish —6G 9
Moorstone Leat. Paign —4F 25
Moor Vw. Bov T & Chud —5B 4
(off Moor La.)
Moorview. Marl —1A 22
Moor Vw. Dri. Teign —2B 8
Moorview End. Marl —1A 22
Moretonhampstead Rd. Lust —1B 4
Morgan Av. Torq —4B 20
Morgans Quay. Shal —6D 8
Morin Rd. Paign —3F 23
Morningside. Daw —6C 2
Mortimer Av. Pres —3E 23
Motehole Rd. Ippn —5B 14
Mt. Boone. Dart —3B 30 (1A 30)
Mt. Boone Hill. Dart —3C 30 (1A 30)
Mt. Boone La. Dart —3B 30 (1A 30)
Mt. Boone Way. Dart —3B 30
Mt. Hermon Rd. Torq —3C 20
Mt. Pleasant Clo. Kgswl —4H 15
Mt. Pleasant La. Shal —6C 8
Mt. Pleasant Rd. Brix —3D 28
Mt. Pleasant Rd. Daw W —1G 3
Mt. Pleasant Rd. Kgswl —4H 15
Mt. Pleasant Rd. New A —3H 11
Mt. Pleasant Rd. Torq —3C 20
Mount Rd. Brix —3E 29
Mount, The. Brix —1D 28
Mount, The. Teign —3D 8
Mount, The. Torq —3E 17
Mount Vw. Ter. Tot —4F 31
(off Grove, The)
Mudstone La. Brix —4E 29
Mulberry Clo. Paign —5B 22
Mulberry St. Teign —4D 8
Murley Cres. Bish —5F 9
Murley Grange. Bish —5F 9
Museum Rd. Torq —5D 20
Musket Rd. Heath —4E 5
Myrtle Hill. Teign —4E 9

Naide Va. Dart —2C 30
Naseby Dri. Heath —4E 5
Nash Gdns. Daw —6D 2
Nelson Clo. Teign —3C 8
Nelson Rd. Brix —2D 28
Nelson Rd. Dart & Town I —3A 30
Nelson Rd. Ind. Est. Dart —4A 30
Ness Dri. Shal —6D 8
Ness Vw. Rd. Teign —1E 9
Netherleigh Rd. Torq —2C 20
Nether Mdw. Marl —6A 18
Netley Rd. New A —1G 11
Neville Rd. New A —1F 11
Newbury Dri. Bov T —3D 4
Newcomen Memorial Engine. —4C 30 (1B 30)
Newcomen Rd. Dart —4C 30 (2B 30)
Newcross Pk. Kgstn —2D 6
Newfoundland Way. New A —2G 11
Newhay Clo. Daw —4C 2
Newhayes. Ippn —6A 14
Newhay, The. Daw —4C 2
Newlands. Daw —3E 3
(in three parts)
New Pk. Bov T —6B 4
New Pk. Clo. Brix —3E 29
New Pk. Cres. Kgstn —3E 7
New Pk. Rd. Kgstn —3E 7
New Pk. Rd. Paign —4C 22
Newport St. Dart —4C 30 (1A 30)
New Quay La. Brix —2E 29
New Quay St. Teign —5D 8
New Rd. Brix —3C 28
New Rd. Sto G —6A 24
New Rd. Teign —3D 8
New Rd. Buckf —4B 32
New St. Paign —5E 23
Newtake Mt. New A —3C 12
Newtake Ri. New A —4C 12
Newton Abbot Racecourse. —6F 7
Newton Abbot Rd. Tot —3G 31
Newton Abbot Town & Great Western Railway Mus. —2H 11
Newton Hill. Dac —1E 17
Newton Rd. Bish —6F 9
Newton Rd. Kgswl —2H 15
Newton Rd. Kgstn —1H 11
Newton Rd. Torq —6B 16
Newton Rd. Bov T & Heath —3B 4
New Wlk. Tot —4G 31
Nicholson Rd. Torq —5C 16
Nightingale Clo. Torq —6D 16
Noelle Dri. New A —1F 11
Norman Clo. New A —6A 6
Norman Rd. Paign —4F 23
N. Boundary Rd. Brix —3B 28
North Embkmt. Dart —4C 30 (1B 30)
N. End Clo. Ippn —5A 14
Northernhay. New A —3H 11
Northfields Ind. Est. Brix —2C 28
Northfields La. Brix —2C 28
Northford Rd. Dart —4B 30 (1A 30)
N. Furzeham Rd. Brix —1D 28
N. Hill Clo. Brix —2C 28
Northleat Av. Paign —6B 22
N. Lodge Clo. Daw —5C 2
N. Rocks Rd. Paign —6E 25
North St. Den —6A 10
North St. Ippn —5B 14
North St. Tot —3F 31
North St. Ashb —3E 33
Northumberland Pl. Teign —5D 8
North Vw. Shal —6C 8
(off Commons Old Rd.)
North Vw. Rd. Brix —2E 29
Northwood La. Buck —1B 32
Nursery Clo. Paign —6D 22
Nursery Rd. Kgstn —4F 7
Nut Bush La. Torq —2E 19
Nut Tree Ct. Brix —5C 28
Nut Tree Orchard. Brix —5C 28

Oak Cliff Chalet Pk. Daw W —1H 3
Oak Cliff Pk. Daw —1H 3
Oak Clo. Kgstn —5G 7
Oakford. Kgstn —4E 7
Oak Hill. Daw —6C 2
Oak Hill Cross Rd. Daw —6B 2
Oak Hill Cross Rd. Teign & Holc —2F 9
Oakhill Rd. Torq —3A 20
Oakland Dri. Daw —5D 2
Oakland Rd. New A —3B 12
Oaklands Clo. Buckf —4A 32
Oaklands Pk. Buckf —3A 32
Oaklands Rd. Buckf —2A 32
Oakland Wlk. Daw —5D 2
Oaklawn Ct. Torq —2A 20
(off St Vincents Rd.)
Oaklawn Ter. Torq —2A 20
(off St Vincents Rd.)
Oakley Clo. Teign —2D 8
Oak Pk. Av. Torq —1G 19
Oak Pk. Clo. Torq —1G 19
Oak Pk. Rd. New A —1E 11
Oak Pk. Vs. Daw —3E 3
Oak Pl. New A —2H 11
Oaks, The. New A —5C 12
Oaks, The. Bov T —3D 4
Oak Tree Dri. New A —5C 12
Oak Tree Gro. Shal —6C 8
Oakymead Pk. Kgstn —5E 7
Oatlands Dri. Paign —1D 24
Occombe Valley Rd. Paign —1D 22
Ocean Vw. Cres. Brix —6B 28
Ocean Vw. Dri. Brix —6B 28
Octon Gro. Torq —2H 19
Oddicombe Beach Hill. Torq —1D 20
Oddicombe Cliff Railway. —1D 20
Odlehill Gro. Abbot —1B 14
Ogwell Mill Rd. New A —3D 10
Ogwell Rd. Ogwl —4D 10
Oke Tor Clo. Paign —1C 22
Old Cider Works La. New A —6F 11
Oldenburg Pk. Paign —4F 23
Old Exeter Rd. New A —1G 11
Old Farm Way. Daw —6D 2
Old Gate Ho. Rd. Daw —3E 3
Old Mkt. Way. Tot —4F 31
Old Mill La. Dart —3A 30
Old Mill Rd. Torq —1H 23
Old Newton Rd. Bov T —5C 4
Old Newton Rd. Heath & Kgswl —1F 15
Old Paignton Rd. Torq —1G 23
(in two parts)
Old Quay St. Teign —5D 8
Old Rd. Galm —2E 27
Old Teignmouth Rd. Daw —6D 2
Old Torquay Rd. Paign —3F 23
Old Torwood Rd. Torq —5D 20
Old Totnes Rd. New A —3F 11
Old Totnes Rd. Buckf —4C 32
Old Totnes Rd. Ashb —5E 33
Old Town St. Daw —4C 2
Old Walls Hill. Teign —1A 8
Oldway Mansion. —3E 23
Oldway Rd. Paign —4E 23
Old Widdicombe La. Paign —4A 22
Old Woods Hill. Torq —2H 19
Old Woods Trad. Est. Torq —1H 19
Orange Gro. Torq —5F 17
Orbec Av. Kgstn —4G 7
Orchard Clo. Brix —4D 28
Orchard Clo. Daw —4D 2
Orchard Clo. Galm —2F 27
Orchard Clo. Kgstn —4G 7
Orchard Clo. Ogwl —4C 10
Orchard Clo. Shal —6B 8
Orchard Clo. Sand —1E 7
Orchard Dri. Ippn —5B 14
Orchard Dri. Kgswl —3G 15
Orchard Gdns. Dart —4B 30
Orchard Gdns. Daw —4D 2
Orchard Gdns. Teign —5E 9
Orchard Gdns. Kgstn —4F 7
Orchard Gro. Brix —5D 28
Orchard Rd. Elcm —3C 20
Orchard Rd. Hele —6E 17
Orchard Rd. Ashb —4F 33
Orchards, The. Galm —2E 27
Orchard Ter. Abbot —6G 11
Orchard Ter. Kgswl —2G 15
Orchard Ter. Tot & Tuck —4F 31
Orchard Ter. Bov T & Chag —2C 4
Orchard Ter. Buckf —4B 32
Orchard, The. Abbot —1B 14
Orchard, The. Bish —5G 9
Orchard, The. Holc —1G 9
Orchard Way. Sto G —5A 24
Orchard Way. Bov T —2C 4
Orchard Waye. Tot —4E 31
Orchid Av. Kgstn —4E 7
Orchid Va. Kgstn —2F 7
Orestone Dri. Maid —2H 17
Orestone La. Dac —4C 16
Orient Rd. Paign —2G 23
Orkney Clo. Torq —5D 16
Orleigh Av. New A —6C 6
Orleigh Pk. New A —6C 6
Orley Rd. Ippn —5A 14
Osbern Rd. Pres —1D 22
Osborn Clo. Ippn —5B 14
Osborne St. New A —2A 12
Osmonds La. Teign —5D 8
(in two parts)
Osmonds M. Teign —5D 8
(off Osmonds La.)
Osney Av. Paign —1E 25
Osney Cres. Paign —1E 25
Osney Gdns. Paign —1E 25
Osprey Dri. Torq —4C 16
Otter Rd. Torq —2F 19

Overclose. *Paign* —3B **22**
Overdale Clo. *Torq* —3E **17**
Overgang. *Brix* —2E **29**
Overgang Rd. *Brix* —1D **28**
Oxenham Grn. *Torq* —3G **19**
Oxford Ct. *Torq* —6E **17**
Oxford La. *Brix* —3B **28**
Oxford St. *Dart* —4C **30** (2B **30**)
Oxlea Clo. *Torq* —5F **21**
Oxlea Rd. *Torq* —5F **21**
Oyster Bend. *Paign* —3F **25**
Oyster Clo. *Paign* —3F **25**

Packhall La. *Brix* —5B **28**
(in two parts)
Padacre Rd. *Torq* —3F **17**
Paddocks, The. *Abbot* —6G **11**
Paddocks, The. *Tot* —3G **31**
Paddock, The. *Daw* —3D **2**
Paddons Coombe. *Kgstn* —2F **7**
Paddons La. *Teign* —2C **8**
(in two parts)
Pafford Av. *Torq* —5G **17**
Pafford Clo. *Torq* —5F **17**
Paige Adams Rd. *Tot* —3E **31**
Paignton & Dartmouth Steam Railway. —2F 25
Paignton Pier. —5G 23
Paignton Rd. *Sto G* —5A **24**
Paignton Zoo Environmental Pk. —1C 24
Palace Av. *Paign* —5E **23**
(in two parts)
Palace Pl. *Paign* —5E **23**
Palatine Clo. *Torq* —4C **20**
Palermo Rd. *Torq* —2D **20**
Palk Clo. *Shal* —6B **8**
Palk St. *Torq* —5C **20**
Palm Rd. *Torq* —4B **20**
Paradise Glen. *Teign* —3D **8**
Paradise Pl. *Brix* —2D **28**
Paradise Rd. *Teign* —3D **8**
Paradise Wlk. *Good* —1F **25**
Paris Rd. *Paign* —3F **23**
Park Av. *Brix* —4C **28**
Park Ct. *Brix* —2F **29**
Parkelands. *Bov T* —3B **4**
Parkers Clo. *Tot* —5G **31**
Parkers Way. *Tot* —5G **31**
Parkfield Clo. *Tot* —4H **31**
Parkfield Clo. *Marl* —6A **18**
Parkfield Rd. *Torq* —2A **20**
Parkham Glade. *Brix* —3D **28**
Parkham La. *Brix* —3D **28**
(in three parts)
Parkham Rd. *Brix* —3D **28**
*Parkham Towers. Brix —3D **28***
(off Wren Hill)
Park Hill. *Teign* —5D **8**
Parkhill Rd. *Torq* —6C **20**
*Park Hill Vs. Teign —5D **8***
(off Park Hill)
Parkhurst Rd. *Torq* —2A **20**
Parkland Cvn. Pk. *Good* —4D **24**
Parklands. *Tot* —3F **31**
(in two parts)
Parklands Way. *Bov T* —6B **4**
Park La. *Torq* —6C **20**
*Park La. Steps. Torq —6D **20***
(off Park La.)
Park M. *Brix* —2F **29**
Park Ri. *Daw* —5D **2**
Park Rd. *Daw* —4D **2**
Park Rd. *Kgswl* —2G **15**
Park Rd. *Torq* —6G **17**
*Park Row Cotts. Daw —4D **2***
(off Stockton Rd.)
Parkside Rd. *Paign* —5F **23**
Park Vw. *New A* —5C **12**
Parson St. *Teign* —4D **8**
Paternoster La. *Ippn* —5A **14**
Pathfields. *Tot* —4G **31**
(in two parts)
Pathfields Clo. *Tot* —4G **31**
Pavilion, The. *Torq* —6C **20**
Pavor Rd. *Torq* —5G **17**
Paynsford Rd. *New A* —1G **11**
Peacock dri. *Paign* —2E **23**
Peak Tor Av. *Torq* —6D **20**
Peaseditch. *Brix* —4E **29**
Peasland Rd. *Torq* —3F **17**
Pebble Ct. *Paign* —1E **25**
*Pellew Arc. Teign —5D **8***
(off Teign St.)
Pellew Way. *Teign* —2C **8**
Pembroke Pk. *Marl* —6B **18**
Pembroke Rd. *Paign* —4B **22**
Pembroke Rd. *Torq* —4C **20**
Pencorse Rd. *Torq* —1A **20**
Pendennis Rd. *Torq* —1A **20**
Penfield Gdns. *Daw* —4C **2**
Penn Inn Clo. *New A* —3B **12**
Penn La. *Brix* —4D **28**
Penn Meadows. *Brix* —4E **29**
Pennsylvania Rd. *Torq* —4C **20**
Pennyacre Rd. *Teign* —3E **9**
Penny's Hill. *Torq* —2A **20**
Penpethy Clo. *Brix* —3C **28**
Penpethy Rd. *Brix* —2C **28**
Penrhyn Pl. *Shal* —6C **8**
Penshurst Rd. *New A* —4G **11**
Pensilva Pk. *Brix* —4D **28**
Pentridge Av. *Torq* —1F **23**
Penwill Way. *Paign* —1C **24**
Peppery La. *Shal* —6B **8**
Peregrine Clo. *Torq* —4C **16**
Perinville Rd. *Torq* —2E **21**
Perros Clo. *Teign* —3B **8**
Peters Cres. *Marl* —6A **18**
Petitor Gdns. *Torq* —6G **17**
Petitor Rd. *Torq* —6G **17**
Petitwell La. *Torq* —6G **17**
Petrel Clo. *Torq* —4B **16**
Picker Head Hill. *Shal* —6C **8**
Pidgley Rd. *Daw* —1F **3**
Piermont Pl. *Daw* —4E **3**
Piers Mus. —5G 23
(off Paignton Pier)
Pillar Av. *Brix* —2C **28**
Pillar Clo. *Brix* —2C **28**
Pillar Cres. *Brix* —2C **28**
Pilmuir Av. *Torq* —4H **19**
Pimlico. *Torq* —4C **20**
Pimm Rd. *Paign* —4B **22**
Pine Clo. *Brix* —5C **28**
Pines Rd. *Paign* —3B **22**
Pine Vw. Av. *Torq* —3D **20**
Pine Vw. Gdns. *Torq* —3D **20**
Pine Vw. Rd. *Torq* —3D **20**
Pinewood Clo. *Daw* —2G **3**
Pinewood Rd. *New A* —3B **12**
Pioneer Ter. *Buckf* —4A **32**
Pipehouse La. *Chud* —1H **5**
Pitland La. *Dac* —1D **16**
Pitley Rd. *Ashb* —3H **33**
Pitt Hill Rd. *New A* —6A **6**
Pitt La. *Daw* —3B **2**
Place La. *Ashb* —2G **33**
Plainmoor Rd. *Torq* —2C **20**
Plains. *Tot* —4G **31**
Plantation Clo. *New A* —4C **12**
Plantation Ter. *Daw* —4D **2**
Plantation Way. *Torq* —5B **16**
Plant World. —6F 13
Platway La. *Shal* —6B **8**
Pleasant Ter. *Paign* —5D **22**
Plym Clo. *Torq* —2E **19**
Plymouth Rd. *Tot* —4E **31**
Plymouth Rd. *Buckf* —6A **32**
Polhearne La. *Brix* —4C **28**
Polhearne Way. *Brix* —4C **28**
Pollyblank Rd. *New A* —2G **11**
Polsham Pk. *Paign* —4E **23**
Pomeroy Av. *Brix* —2B **28**
Pomeroy Rd. *New A* —2F **11**
Pook La. *Ashb* —3F **33**
Poplar Clo. *Brix* —6A **28**
Poplar Clo. *New A* —5C **12**
Poplars Dri. *Marl* —1A **22**
Poplars, The. *Chud* —1H **5**
Poplar Ter. *Ippn* —5B **14**
Porlock Way. *Paign* —3C **24**
Port Hill. *Galm* —2D **26**
Portland Av. *Teign* —2E **9**
Portland Rd. *Torq* —2E **21**
Potters Hill. *Torq* —4C **20**
Pottery Clo. *Bov T* —5B **4**
Pottery Ct. *Dart* —3A **30**
Pottery Rd. *Kgstn* —5E **7**
Pottery Rd. *Bov T* —5B **4**
Pound Fld. *Sto G* —5A **24**
Pound La. *Kgswl* —3G **15**
Pound La. *Shal* —6A **8**
Pound La. *Teign* —5E **9**
Pound Pl. *Bov T* —2C **4**
Poundsgate Clo. *Brix* —3F **29**
Powderham Clo. *New A* —3G **11**
Powderham Rd. *New A* —2G **11**
Powderham Rd. *Torq* —6E **17**
Powderham Ter. *New A* —3G **11**
Powderham Ter. *Teign* —5E **9**
Preston Down Av. *Pres* —1E **23**
Preston Down Rd. *Paign & Pres* —6B **18**
Prigg Mdw. *Ashb* —4F **33**
Primley Ct. *Paign* —6B **22**
Primley Pk. *Paign* —6C **22**
Primley Pk. E. *Paign* —6D **22**
Primrose Clo. *Kgstn* —4F **7**
Primrose Way. *Kgswl* —1G **15**
Prince Charles Ct. *Torq* —4F **17**
Prince of Wales Dri. *Dart* —3C **30**
Prince Rupert Way. *Heath* —4F **5**
Princes Rd. *Torq* —4C **20**
Princes Rd. E. *Torq* —4D **20**
Princes Rd. W. *Torq* —4C **20**
Princess Pde. *Torq* —6C **20**
Princess Rd. *Kgswl* —3H **15**
Princess Rd. *Kgstn* —3E **7**
Prince's St. *Daw* —4D **2**
Princes St. *Paign* —5E **23**
Princes St. *Torq* —2E **21**
Prince St. *New A* —2H **11**
Prince William Ct. *Brix* —3D **28**
*Prings Ct. Brix —2D **28***
(off Market St.)
Priory. *Bov T* —2B **4**
Priory Av. *Kgswl* —2H **15**
Priory Av. *Tot* —3F **31**
Priory Ct. *Tot* —4F **31**
Priory Dri. *Tot* —3F **31**
Priory Gdns. *Daw* —4E **3**
Priory Gdns. *Tot* —3F **31**
Priory Ga. *Tot* —3F **31**
Priory Hill. *Daw* —4E **3**
Priory Hill. *Tot* —3F **31**
Priory Pk. Rd. *Daw* —4D **2**
Priory Rd. *Abbot* —1C **14**
Priory Rd. *Daw* —4E **3**
Priory Rd. *Torq* —1C **20**
Priory St. *Kgswr* —5D **30**
*Priory Ter. Tot —3F **31***
(off Priory Hill)
Priscott Way. *Kgstn* —5F **7**
Promenade. *Good* —1F **25**
Promenade. *Paign* —3G **23**
Promenade. *Broads* —6G **25**
Promenade. *Teign* —5E **9**
Prospect Rd. *Brix* —2D **28**
Prospect Ter. *New A* —2H **11**
Puddavine Ter. *Tot* —1E **31**
Pump St. *Brix* —2E **29**
Purbeck Av. *Torq* —1F **23**

Quantocks Rd. *Torq* —6F **19**
Quarry Gdns. *Paign* —4D **22**
Quay Rd. *New A* —2A **12**
(in two parts)
Quay Rd. *Teign* —5D **8**
Quay Ter. *New A* —2A **12**
Quay, The. *Brix* —2E **29**
Quay, The. *Dart* —4C **30** (1B **30**)
Quay, The. *Dit* —5A **26**
Quaywest Leisure Pk. —2F 25
Queen Annes Copse. *New A* —4E **11**
Queen Elizabeth Av. *Dart* —3B **30**
Queen Elizabeth Dri. *Paign* —5B **22**
Queen La. *Daw* —4D **2**
Queens Clo. *Kgstn* —3G **7**
Queen's Cres. *Brix* —4E **29**
Queen's Pk. Rd. *Paign* —5F **23**
Queen's Rd. *Brix* —1D **28**
Queen's Rd. *Paign* —5F **23**
Queen's Ter. *Tot* —3F **31**
Queen St. *Daw* —4D **2**
Queen St. *New A* —2H **11**
Queen St. *Teign* —5D **8**
Queen St. *Torq* —4C **20**
Queensway. *New A* —3B **12**
Queensway. *Torq* —3G **19**
Queensway Clo. *Torq* —2H **19**
Queensway Cres. *Torq* —2H **19**
Queensway Ho. *New A* —3B **12**
Quentin Av. *Brix* —5C **28**
Quinta Clo. *Torq* —3D **20**
Quinta Ct. *Torq* —2D **20**
Quinta Rd. *Torq* —3D **20**

Raddicombe Dri. *Brix* —6A **28**
Radley Gdns. *Bish* —5H **9**
Radnor Ter. *Tot* —3F **31**
Radway Gdns. *Bish* —5H **9**
Radway Hill. *Bish* —5H **9**
Radway St. *Bish* —5H **9**
Rainbow Ct. *Torq* —2H **19**
Raleigh Av. *Torq* —3G **19**
Raleigh Clo. *Dart* —4A **30**
Raleigh Dri. *Good* —3E **25**
Raleigh Rd. *Dart* —3B **30**
Raleigh Rd. *New A* —2C **12**
Raleigh Rd. *Teign* —2C **8**
Raleigh St. *Dart* —4C **30** (1B **30**)
Ramshill Rd. *Paign* —3B **22**
Randolph Ct. *New A* —1F **11**
Rangers Clo. *Buckf* —5B **32**
Ranscombe Clo. *Brix* —2F **29**
Ranscombe Rd. *Brix* —2E **29**
Rathmore Rd. *Torq* —5H **19**
(in three parts)
Ravensbury Dri. *Dart* —5D **30**
Rawlyn Rd. *Torq* —5G **19**
Rea Barn Clo. *Brix* —3E **29**
Rea Barn Rd. *Brix* —3E **29**
Rea Dri. *Brix* —2E **29**
Rectory Field Nature Reserve. —5D 10
Rectory Rd. *Ogwl* —4D **10**
Redavon Ri. *Torq* —1E **19**
Red Brook Clo. *Paign* —4F **25**
Redburn Clo. *Paign* —4D **22**
Redburn Rd. *Paign* —4D **22**

Redcliffe Rd. Torq —6H 17
Reddenhill Rd. Torq —3D 20
Redgate Clo. Torq —3E 21
Red Ho. Clo. Chud —1H 5
Redlands Ct. Paign —4C 22
Redoubt Hill. Kgswr —4D 30
Redstart Clo. New A —4E 11
Redwalls Mdw. Dart —3B 30
Redwell La. Paign —3C 22
Redwell Rd. Paign —3C 22
Redwoods. Bov T —5B 4
Redworth Ter. Tot —3F 31
Reed Va. Teign —4C 8
Reeves Clo. Tot —4G 31
(off New Wlk.)
Reeves Rd., The. Torq —4G 19
Regent Clo. Torq —1H 19
Regent Gdns. Teign —5E 9
(off Regent St.)
Regent St. Daw —4D 2
Regent St. Teign —5E 9
Rendells Mdw. Bov T —3D 4
Rewlea Cotts. Ashb —2F 33
Rew Rd. Ashb —1F 33
(in two parts)
Reynell Av. New A —2C 12
Reynell Rd. Ogwl —5E 11
Rhine Vs. Tot —4G 31
Rhodanthe Rd. Paign —2E 23
Richards Clo. Daw —5D 2
Richmond Clo. Torq —4H 21
Richmond Ct. Daw —4E 3
(off Richmond Pl.)
Richmond Ct. Paign —4E 23
Richmond Hill. Kgswl —2H 15
Richmond Pl. Daw —4E 3
Ridge Hill. Dart —3C 30
Ridge La. Comp —1C 18
Ridgemark Clo. Brix —2F 29
Ridge Rd. Maid —1G 17
Ridge Rd. Neth —2G 13
Ridges, The. Dart —5A 30
Ridgeway Clo. New A —4C 12
Ridgeway Heights. Torq —5E 21
Ridgeway Hill. Comp —3A 18
Ridgeway La. Cof —1B 16
Ridgeway Rd. New A —4B 12
Ridgeway Rd. Torq —6E 21
Ridley Hill. Kgswr —5D 30
Rillage La. Torq —3A 20
Ringmore Clo. Shal —6B 8
Ringmore Rd. Shal —6A 8
Ringslade Clo. New A —6A 6
Ringslade Rd. New A —5A 6
Rippon Clo. Brix —5A 28
Riverside. Shal —6C 8
Riverside. Tot —2E 31
Riverside Ct. New A —1A 12
Riverside Mill. —3B 4
(Devon Guild of Craftsmen, The)
Riverside Rd. Dit —4A 26
Riverview. New A —3C 12
Riviera Ter. Daw —3F 3
Riviera, The. Paign —6E 23
Riviera Way. Torq —6A 16
Robers Rd. Kgstn —3E 7
Roberts Clo. Torq —5G 17
Roberts Way. New A —1E 11
Roborough La. Ashb —3F 33
Roborough Ter. Ashb —3F 33
Rock Clo. Paign —6F 25
Rock End Av. Torq —6D 20
Rockfield Clo. Teign —2F 9
Rock Ho. La. Maid —3H 17
Rock La. Teign —3C 8
(in three parts)
Rock Pk. Dart —3A 30
Rock Pk. Ashb —2G 33
Rock Rd. Torq —5C 20
Rockstone, The. Daw —3G 3
Rock Wlk. Torq —5B 20
Rocky La. Buckf —6A 32
Rocombe Clo. Torq —3E 17
Rocombe Hill. New A —6H 13
Rodgers Ind. Est. Paign —2A 24
Rodney Clo. Dart —4A 30
Rogada Ct. Brix —5E 29
Romaleyn Gdns. Paign —1E 25
Rooklands Av. Torq —2A 20
Rope Wlk. Teign —4D 8
Ropewalk Hill. Brix —2D 28
Rose Acre Ter. Brix —3E 29
Rose Dene. Torq —5E 17
Rose Hill. Kgswl —3G 15
Rosehill Clo. Torq —4D 20
Rose Hill Clo. Kgswl —3G 15
Rosehill Gdns. Kgswl —3G 15
Rosehill Rd. Torq —4C 20
Roselands Dri. Paign —2B 24
Roseland Sq. Kgstn —4F 7
Roselands Rd. Paign —2C 24
Rosemary Av. New A —1E 11
Rosemary Ct. Paign —3E 23
Rosemary Gdns. Paign —3C 22
Rosery Rd. Torq —4H 19
Roseville St. Dart —4C 30 (1A 30)
Rosewarne Av. New A —3C 12
Rossall Dri. Paign —6D 22
Rosyl Av. Holc —1G 9
Rotherfold. Tot —4E 31
Rougemont Av. Torq —6B 16
Roundham Av. Paign —1G 25
Roundham Cres. Paign —6G 23
Roundham Gdns. Paign —1F 25
Roundham Rd. Paign —6F 23
Roundhead Rd. Heath —3E 5
Roundhill Rd. Torq —1G 23
Roundings, The. Galm —2E 27
Roundmoors Clo. Kgswl —5H 15
Roundway, The. Kgswl —1G 15
Rousdown Rd. Torq —5H 19
Rowan Clo. Ogwl —4E 11
Rowantree Rd. New A —4B 12
Rowan Way. Brix —5A 28
Rowbrook Clo. Paign —2B 24
Rowcroft Rd. Paign —3F 23
Rowdens Rd. Torq —4A 20
Rowdens, The. Teign —3E 9
Rowley Rd. Torq —1C 20
Rowsell's La. Tot —4G 31
Royal Pines. Torq —6E 21
Ruckamore Rd. Torq —4H 19
Rundle Rd. New A —1H 11
Rushlade Clo. Paign —3C 24
Rush Way. Tot —4H 31
Russell Ct. Tot —4F 31
(off Victoria St.)
Russets La. Buck —3C 32
Ryde Clo. Torq —5F 17
Rydon Acres. Kgstn —3F 7
Rydon Acres. Sto G —5A 24
Rydon Av. Kgstn —3F 7
Rydon Est. Kgstn —3F 7
Rydon Ind. Est. Kgstn —5E 7
Rydon La. Abbot —1D 14
Rydon Path. Kgstn —2F 7
Rydon Rd. Kgstn —2F 7
Rydons. Brix —3B 28

Sabre Clo. Heath —3E 5
Saddle, The. Paign —3F 25
St Agnes La. Torq —6H 19
St Albans Rd. Torq —2D 20
St Andrews Clo. Ashb —4F 33
St Andrews Rd. Paign —6F 23
St Anne's Ct. New A —2F 11
St Anne's Rd. Torq —2D 20
St Augustine's Clo. Torq —4F 17
St Bartholomew Way. Ogwl —4C 10
St Bernard's Clo. Buck —2B 32
(in two parts)
St Catherine's Rd. Torq —1C 20
St Clements Ct. Dart —3A 30
(off Church Rd.)
St David's Rd. Teign —1D 8
St Dominics Clo. Torq —1C 20
St Edmund's Rd. Torq —2C 20
(in two parts)
St Efride's Rd. Torq —4A 20
St Georges Cres. Torq —2D 20
St George's Rd. Torq —2D 20
St Ives Ct. Torq —3B 20
St James Pl. Torq —2E 21
St James Rd. Torq —2B 20
St James's Ho. Teign —4D 8
(off Fore St.)
St James's Precinct. Teign —4D 8
(off Bitton Pk. Rd.)
St John's Clo. Bish —6G 9
St John's Clo. Bov T —4B 4
St John's Ct. Tot —4G 31
(off Weston Rd.)
St Johns La. Bov T —3B 4
St Johns Pl. Torq —5C 20
(off Braddons Hill Rd. W.)
St Johns St. New A —1H 11
St John's Ter. Tot —3E 31
(off Station Rd.)
St Katherine's M. Tot —4F 31
(off St Katherine's Way)
St Katherine's Rd. Torq —3H 19
St Katherine's Way. Tot —4F 31
St Lawrence La. Ashb —4F 33
St Leonard's Clo. New A —3G 11
St Leonard's Rd. New A —3G 11
St Leonard's Tower. —2G 11
(off Courtenay Street)
St Luke's Clo. New A —4C 12
St Luke's Pk. Torq —5B 20
St Luke's Rd. New A —4B 12
St Luke's Rd. Torq —4B 20
St Luke's Rd. N. Torq —5B 20
St Luke's Rd. S. Torq —5B 20
St Margaret's Av. Torq —2C 20
St Margaret's Clo. Torq —1C 20
St Margaret's Rd. Torq —1C 20
St Mark's Rd. Torq —6E 21
St Martins Ct. Torq —6E 17
St Marychurch Rd. Coff & New A —3B 12
St Marychurch Rd. Torq —6G 17
St Mary's Bay Holiday Cen. Brix —4F 29
St Marys Clo. Abbot —1B 14
St Mary's Clo. Brix —5C 28
St Marys Ct. New A —2G 11
(off Highweek St.)
St Mary's Ct. Paign —5D 22
St Mary's Orchid Paradise. —4A 6
St Mary's Pk. Paign —1A 24
St Mary's Rd. Brix —5D 28
St Mary's Rd. New A —3G 11
St Mary's Rd. Teign —2C 8
St Mary's Sq. Brix —4C 28
St Matthew's Rd. Torq —5G 19
St Matthias Chu. Rd. Torq —4F 21
St Mawes Dri. Paign —5E 25
St Michaels. New A —3H 11
(off Courtenay Rd.)
St Michael's Clo. Torq —3H 19
St Michael's Rd. Kgstn —5E 7
St Michael's Rd. New A —4A 12
St Michael's Rd. Paign —6D 22
St Michael's Rd. Teign —2E 9
St Michael's Rd. Torq —2H 19
St Michael's Ter. Torq —4C 20
St Pauls Clo. Bov T —3C 4
St Paul's Ct. New A —2H 11
(off Oak Pl.)
St Paul's Cres. Torq —2C 20
St Paul's Rd. New A —2H 11
St Paul's Rd. Paign —2G 23
St Paul's Rd. Torq —2C 20
St Peter's Clo. Bov T —2D 4
St Peters Clo. Torq —3G 19
St Peter's Hill. Brix —2E 29
St Peter's Quay. Tot —5G 31
St Thomas Clo. Bov T —3D 4
St Vincent's Clo. Torq —3A 20
St Vincent's Rd. Torq —2A 20
Salem Pl. New A —2G 11
Salisbury Av. Torq —5E 17
Salisbury Rd. New A —1A 12
Salisbury Ter. Teign —4E 9
Saltern Rd. Paign —4F 25
Saltings, The. Shal —6B 8
Salty La. Shal —6B 8
Sanders Rd. Brix —2B 28
Sandford Vw. New A —1G 11
Sand La. Tot —1H 31
Sandown Rd. Paign —3C 24
Sandpath Rd. Kgstn —5F 7
Sandquay Rd. Dart —2C 30
Sandringham Dri. Pres —1D 22
Sandringham Gdns. Pres —1E 23
Sandringham Rd. New A —2B 12
Sands Ct. Paign —6E 23
Sands Rd. Paign —6F 23
Sandygate. Kgstn —2D 6
Sandygate Mill. Kgstn —1E 7
Sandy La. Daw —2F 3
Sanford Rd. Torq —4H 19
San Remo Ter. Daw —4F 3
Saturday's La. Kgswl —6G 15
Sawyer Dri. Teign —2B 8
Saxon Heights. Brix —3D 28
Saxon Mdw. Paign —6A 22
Scarborough Pl. Torq —4A 20
Scarborough Rd. Torq —4A 20
School Board Steps. Dart —2A 30
School Cotts. Tgnrc —3B 6
School Ct. Dart —4A 30
School Hill. Daw —4D 2
School Hill. Sto G —6A 24
School Hill Cotts. Sto G —6A 24
School La. Shal —6C 8
School Rd. Kgswl —2G 15
School Rd. New A —2H 11
School Rd. Tngrc —3A 6
Scoresby Clo. Torq —3G 17
Scratton Path. Ogwl —5E 11
(off Reynell Rd.)
Screechers Hill. Ashb —3E 33
Sea La. Brix —3F 29
Sea Lawn Ter. Daw —3F 3
(off Exeter Rd.)
Seale Clo. Dart —3A 30
(off Mill Cres.)
Seaton Clo. Torq —2E 21
Seaview Cres. Pres —2F 23
Sea Vw. Ter. Brix —1D 28
(off Overgang Rd.)
Seaway Clo. Torq —6H 19
Seaway Ct. Brix —3C 28
Seaway Ct. Torq —6A 20
Seaway Cres. Paign —3G 23
Seaway Gdns. Paign —3G 23
Seaway Holiday Pk. Daw —1F 3
Seaway La. Torq —5G 19
Seaway Rd. Paign —3F 23
Secmaton La. Daw —2E 3
Secmaton Ri. Daw —1E 3

Second Av. Daw —5C 2
Second Av. Teign —4C 8
Second Av. Torq —1B 20
Second Dri. Teign —3F 9
(Dawlish Rd.)
Second Dri. Teign —4D 8
(Yannon Dri.)
Sefton Ct. Torq —2E 21
Sellick Av. Brix —4E 29
Sett Clo. Bov T —3C 4
Severn Rd. Torq —2E 19
Seymour Dri. Torq —3F 17
Seymour Pl. Tot —4G 31
Seymour Rd. Tot —4G 31
Seymour Rd. New A —1G 11
Shadynook Cvn. Site. Kgstn —4F 7
Shaftesbury Clo. Daw —4D 2
Shaftesbury Pl. Tot —4F 31
(off Maudlin Rd.)
Shakespeare Clo. Torq —3G 19
Shaldon Bri. Teign —5C 8
Shaldon Rd. Combe —1H 13
Shaldon Rd. New A —3B 12
Shaldon Rd. Shal —6A 8
Shapley Tor Clo. Brix —5B 28
Shaptor Vw. Bov T —5A 4
Sharkham Point Cvn. Pk. Brix —5E 29
Sharpham Dri. Tot —5F 31
Sharpitor Clo. Paign —2C 22
Sharp's Clo. Heath —4F 5
Sharp's Crest. Heath —4F 5
Shearwater Dri. Torq —4C 16
Shedden Hill Rd. Torq —5B 20
Shelley Av. Torq —1B 20
Shelston Tor Dri. Paign —2C 24
Shepherd Clo. Paign —6B 22
Shepherd's La. Bish —1A 8
Sherborne Rd. New A —2G 11
Sherwell Hill. Torq —4G 19
Sherwell La. Torq —4G 19
Sherwell Pk. Rd. Torq —4G 19
Sherwell Ri. S. Torq —4G 19
Sherwell Valley Rd. Torq —3F 19
Shetland Clo. Torq —5D 16
Shillingate Clo. Daw —6C 2
Shiphay Av. Torq —2F 19
Shiphay La. Torq —1F 19
Shiphay Mnr. Dri. Torq —2G 19
Shiphay Pk. Rd. Torq —2G 19
Shirburn Rd. Torq —2B 20
Shire Clo. Paign —5D 24
Shirley Towers. Torq —6C 20
Shobbrook Hill. New A —1D 10
Shorland Clo. Daw —2F 3
Shorton Rd. Paign & Pres —2D 22
(in two parts)
Shorton Valley Rd. Paign —2D 22
Shrewsbury Av. Torq —6F 17
Shute Hill. Bish —5H 9
Shute Hill. Teign —4E 9
Shute Hill Cres. Teign —4E 9
Shute Rd. Tot —4G 31
Shutterton Ind. Est. Daw —1F 3
Sidney Ct. Daw —4D 2
(off Old Town St.)
Sidney Wlk. Good —4E 25
Silver Bri. Clo. Paign —5F 25
Silverhills Rd. Dec I —5A 12
Silver St. Ippn —6A 14
Silver St. Buckf —4B 32
Silverwood Av. New A —4B 12
Singer Clo. Paign —6D 22
Singmore Rd. Marl —1B 22
Skye Clo. Torq —5D 16
Slade La. Abbot —1B 14
(in two parts)
Slade La. Galm —2E 27
Sladnor Pk. Rd. Maid —2G 17
Slanns Mdw. Kgstn —5E 7
Sleepy La. Paign —2D 22
Smallcombe Rd. Paign —3B 22
Smalldon La. Torq —4G 17
Smallwell La. Marl —1A 22
Smardon Av. Brix —2B 28
Smardon Clo. Brix —2B 28
Smith Hill. Bish —5G 9
Smith St. Dart —4C 30 (1A 30)
Smugglers La. Daw —1H 9
Snowberry Clo. Torq —2A 20
Solomon's Post Cvn. & Camp Site. Torq —1G 17
Solsbro M. Torq —5H 19
Solsbro Rd. Torq —5H 19
Somerset Pl. Teign —5D 8
Somerset Pl. Tot —4G 31
Soper Rd. Teign —2C 8
Soper Wlk. Teign —2C 8
Sophia Way. New A —3F 11
Sorrell Ct. Kgstn —4E 7
S. Bay Holiday Camp. Brix —5E 29
Southbrook Clo. Bov T —2B 4
Southbrook La. Bov T —2A 4
Southbrook Rd. Bov T —2B 4
Southcote Orchard. Tot —4H 31
S. Devon Coast Path. Shal —6D 8
South Devon Railway Mus. —4D 32
Southdown Av. Brix —5C 28
Southdown Clo. Brix —5C 28
Southdown Hill. Brix —5C 28
Southdown Rd. Brix —6C 28
S. Downs Rd. Daw —6D 2
South Embkmt. Dart —4C 30 (2B 30)
Southern Clo. Torq —3F 17
Southernhay. New A —3H 11
Southey Cres. Kgswl —4H 15
Southey Dri. Kgswl —4H 15
Southey La. Kgswl —3H 15
Southfield Av. Pres —2C 22
Southfield Clo. Pres —3C 22
Southfield Ri. Paign —4D 22
Southfield Rd. Paign —4D 22
S. Ford Rd. Dart —4B 30 (2A 30)
S. Furzeham Rd. Brix —2D 28
S. Hill Rd. Torq —5D 20
Southlands Rd. Torq —4A 20
S. Parks Rd. Torq —5E 17
South Quay. Harb T —6F 23
South Rd. New A —4G 11
South St. Torq —4A 20
South St. Tot —4F 31
Southtown. Dart —5C 30
South Vw. Abbot —1C 14
South Vw. Teign —5D 8
Southview Rd. Paign —4D 22
Southway Av. Torq —6E 17
Southwood Ct. Torq —4D 20
Sovereign M. Torq —5G 17
Sparks Barn Rd. Paign —1D 24
Sparrow Rd. Tot —4E 31
Speedwell Clo. Brix —4D 28
Spencer Rd. New A —3H 11
Spencer Rd. Paign —5B 22
(in three parts)
Speranzo Gro. Teign —4D 8
(off Exeter St.)
Spring Clo. New A —1D 10
Springdale Clo. Brix —5D 28
Springfield. Ippn —6B 14
Springfield Gdns. Daw —1F 3
Springfield Rd. Torq —2C 20
Springhill Rd. Tot —4H 31
Spruce Way. Paign —3B 22
Square, The. Kgswr —4D 30
Stabb Clo. Paign —4D 24
Stabb Dri. Paign —4D 24
Stables, The. Tot —3G 31
Staddons Lea La. Torq —3F 19
Staddons Vw. Bov T —2B 4
Stadium Dri. Kgswl —5H 15
Stafford Ct. Tot —4H 31
Stafford Rd. Paign —6F 23
Stanbury Rd. Torq —2F 19
Stanley Gdns. Paign —4C 22
Stanley Rd. Torq —1D 20
Stanley St. Teign —5D 8
Stanmore Ri. Daw —3E 3
Stanmore Tor. Paign —6D 22
Stansfeld Av. Paign —5D 22
Stantaway Pk. Torq —2A 20
Stantor La. Marl —3C 18
Stapledon La. Ashb —3F 33
Stapleton Clo. Paign —2B 24
Starpitten Gro. Torq —4G 17
Starpitten La. W. Torq —5F 17
Start Av. Teign —2E 9
Station Hill. Brix —2D 28
Station La. Paign —6E 23
Station Rd. Daw —4E 3
Station Rd. New A —2A 12
Station Rd. Teign —5E 9
Station Rd. Tot —3F 31
Station Rd. Bov T —3B 4
Station Rd. Buckf —4C 32
Steamer Quay Rd. Tot —4G 31
Steartfield Rd. Paign —4F 23
Steed Clo. Paign —5D 24
Steep Hill. Maid —1H 17
Stella Rd. Paign —2D 22
Stentiford Hill Rd. Torq —4C 20
Steppes Mdw. New A —3F 11
Steps La. Torq —4G 17
(in two parts)
Stitchill Rd. Torq —5D 20
Stockmeadow Gdns. Bish —6H 9
Stockton Av. Daw —4D 2
Stockton Cotts. Daw —4D 2
(off School Hill)
Stockton Hill. Daw —4D 2
Stockton La. Daw —4D 2
(off Stockton Rd.)
Stockton Rd. Daw —4D 2
Stoke Gabriel Rd. Galm —1B 26
Stoke Hill. Sto G —6A 24
Stokeinteignhead Rd. Torq —1H 17
Stoke Rd. Paign —2A 24
Stoneacre Clo. Brix —4D 28
Stone Ct. Torq —6C 16
Stonelands Pk. Daw —4C 2
Stonelands Ter. Daw —4C 2
Stoneleigh Clo. New A —1E 11
Stoneleigh Dri. Torq —6G 19
Stoneman's Hill. Abbot —5G 11
Stone Pk. Paign —1G 27
Stonepark. Ashb —5E 33
Stonepark Cres. Ashb —5E 33
Stonepark Ter. Ashb —5E 33
Stones Clo. Kgstn —2F 7
Stoneyhill. Abbot —4B 14
Storrs Clo. Bov T —2B 4
Stover Country Pk. & Ranger's Office Info. Cen. —5F 5
Strand. Shal —6C 8
Strand. Teign —5D 8
Strand. Torq —5C 20
Strand Hill. Daw —4E 3
Strand, The. Brix —2E 29
Strand, The. Daw —4E 3
Strand, The. Shal —6A 8
Strap La. Kgstn —2E 7
Strawberry Ter. Kgstn —3F 7
Stringland La. Comp —4A 18
Strode Rd. Buckf —5B 32
Stuart Ct. Daw —6D 2
Studley Rd. Torq —2B 20
Sturcombe Av. Paign —2B 24
Sugar Loaf & Saltern Cove Nature Reserve. —4F 25
Summercourt Way. Brix —5A 28
Summerfield Rd. Torq —1H 19
Summerhayes. Daw —6D 2
Summerland Av. Daw —3D 2
Summerland Clo. Daw —4D 2
Summerland Cotts. New A
(off Carlisle St.) —2H 11
Summerland Ct. New A —2H 11
Summerlands Clo. Brix —5B 28
Summerlands Ct. Brix —5B 28
Summer La. Brix —4B 28
Summer La. Tgnrc —6H 5
Summers Fld. Ct. Paign —6F 23
Sunbury Hill. Torq —3B 20
Sunbury Rd. Paign —6E 23
Sun Ct. New A —2G 11
Suncrest Cvn. Site. Torq —4E 17
Suncrest Clo. Torq —5E 17
Sun La. Teign —5D 8
Sunnybank. Abbot —1C 14
Sunny Clo. New A —2C 12
Sunny Hollow. Ogwl —5C 10
Sunnymead Ter. Tot —4F 31
(off Maudlin Rd.)
Sunnyside Rd. Kgswl —4H 15
Sun Valley Clo. Brix —2D 28
Sussex Clo. Torq —4F 17
Sutherland Clo. New A —5C 12
Sutherland Rd. Torq —4D 20
Sutton Clo. Daw —3D 2
Sutton Clo. Torq —3E 17
Swale Clo. Torq —4F 17
Swallowfield Ri. Torq —5B 16
Swallowfields. Tot —2E 31
Swallows Acre. Daw —3E 3
Swanborough Rd. New A —4C 12
Swan Ct. Dart —4B 30
(off Victoria Rd.)
Swannaton Rd. Dart —6B 30
Swedwell Rd. Torq —3F 17
Sweetbriar Clo. Holc —1G 9
Sweetbriar La. Holc —1G 9
Swift Ind. Est. Kgstn —5E 7
Swincombe Dri. Paign —5C 22
Sycamore Clo. Paign —6G 25
Sycamore Way. Brix —5B 28
Symons Pas. Tot —4G 31

Tamar Av. Torq —2E 19
Tamwyn Clo. Paign —3F 23
Tanners Rd. Good & Paign —1F 25
Tapley Gdns. Bish —5H 9
Tarraway Rd. Paign —2G 23
Tarr's Av. Kgstn —4F 7
Tarrs End. Kgstn —4F 7
Tarr's La. Kgstn —4F 7
Taunton Ct. Tot —4G 31
(off New Wlk.)
Tavis Rd. Paign —3C 22
Tavistock Pl. Paign —5E 25
Tavy Av. Torq —1E 19
Taylor Clo. Daw —5C 2
Teign Clo. Bish —5F 9
Teignfield Cvn. Site. Shal —6A 8
Teignmouth Hill. Daw —5E 3
Teignmouth Lifeboat Station. —6D 8
Teignmouth Mus. —4E 9
Teignmouth Rd. Bish —6H 9
(in two parts)

Teignmouth Rd. *Daw* —6D **2**
Teignmouth Rd. *Kgstn* —4G **7**
Teignmouth Rd. *Teign & Daw* —2F **9**
Teignmouth Rd. *Maid & Torq* —2A **20**
Teign Rd. *New A* —2A **12**
Teign St. *Teign* —5D **8**
Teign Vw. *Chud* —1H **5**
Teign Vw. Pl. *Teign* —5D **8**
Teignview Rd. *Bish* —5G **9**
Tembani Ct. *Paign* —4F **23**
*Temperance Pl. Brix —2E **29***
(off King St.)
Temperance St. *Torq* —4B **20**
Templar Way. *Tgnrc* —1A **6**
Templer Rd. *Pres* —6D **18**
Templer's Rd. *New A* —1A **12**
Templer's Way. *Kgstn* —2E **7**
Tennyson Clo. *Torq* —1B **20**
Terrace, The. *Torq* —5C **20**
Terrace Wlk. *Ashb* —3F **33**
Thatcher Av. *Torq* —6G **21**
Thatcher Dri. *Teign* —1E **9**
Thatcher Heights. *Torq* —6G **21**
Third Av. *Daw* —5D **2**
Third Av. *Teign* —4C **8**
Third Av. *Torq* —1B **20**
Third Dri. *Teign* —4D **8**
Thomas Newcombe Ct. Dart
*(off Ivatt Rd.) —4A **30***
Thorncliff Clo. *Torq* —4F **21**
Thorn Clo. *New A* —1D **10**
Thorne Pk. Rd. *Torq* —4G **19**
Thornley Dri. *Teign* —4C **8**
Throgmorton Ho. *Tot* —4G **31**
Thrushel Clo. *Brix* —5B **28**
*Thurlestone Ct. Dart —4B **30***
(off Victoria Rd.)
Thurlestone Gdns. *Dart* —4B **30**
Thurlestone Rd. *New A* —1G **11**
Thurlow Hill. *Torq* —3B **20**
Thurlow Pk. *Torq* —3B **20**
Thurlow Rd. *Torq* —3B **20**
Ticklemore St. *Tot* —4G **31**
Timbers Clo. *Buckf* —6A **32**
Timbers Rd. *Buckf* —6A **32**
Timber Ter. *Kgswl* —3G **15**
Times M. *Tot* —4F **31**
Tintagel Clo. *Torq* —1A **20**
Titchfield Gdns. *Paign* —4C **22**
*Tollit Gdns. Tot —4G **31***
(off Weston Rd.)
Top Cliff Rd. *Shal* —6B **8**
(in two parts)
Torbay Ct. *Brix* —2F **29**
Torbay Holiday Chalets. *Brix* —1C **28**
Torbay Rd. *Paign* —5F **23**
Torbay Rd. *Torq* —2G **23**
Tor Chu. Rd. *Torq* —4A **20**
Tor Clo. *Paign* —6E **25**
Tor Gdns. *Ogwl* —4C **10**
Tor Hill Rd. *Torq* —4A **20**
Tor Pk. Rd. *Paign* —2A **24**
Tor Pk. Rd. *Torq* —3A **20**
Torquay Holiday Village. *Torq* —4C **16**
Torquay Mus. —5D 20
Torquay Rd. *Kgswl* —3H **15**
Torquay Rd. *New A* —2H **11**
Torquay Rd. *Paign* —5E **23**
Torquay Rd. *Shal* —6C **8**
Torre Abbey. —5A 20
Torridge Av. *Torq* —2E **19**
Tors, The. *Kgswl* —3G **15**
Tor Va. *Torq* —3A **20**
Tor View. *Buckf* —5A **32**
Tor Vw. Av. *New A* —3C **12**
Tor Vw. Gdns. *Paign* —5D **22**
Torwood Clo. *Torq* —6D **20**
Torwood Ct. *Torq* —5E **21**
Torwood Gdns. Rd. *Torq* —6D **20**
Torwood Mt. *Torq* —5D **20**
Torwood St. *Torq* —5D **20**
Tothill Ct. *Shal* —6C **8**
Totnes Castle. —4F 31
Totnes Costume Mus. —4F 31
(Devonshire Collection of Period Costume)
Totnes Down Hill. *Tot* —5F **31**
Totnes Guildhall. —4F 31
Totnes Ind. Est. *Tot* —2G **31**
Totnes Mus. —4F 31
(Elizabethan)
Totnes Rd. *New A* —6F **11**
Totnes Rd. *Ippn & Abbot* —6B **14**
Totnes Rd. *Paign* —6A **22**
Totnes Rd. *Torq* —6D **18**
Totnes Rd. *Buckf* —4D **32**
Totnes Rd. *Marl & Paign* —2A **22**
Tourist Info. Cen. —3B 4
(Bovey Tracey)
Tourist Info. Cen. —2E 29
(Brixham)
Tourist Info. Cen.
(Dartmouth) —4C 30 (1B 30)
Tourist Info. Cen. —2G 11
(Newton Abbot)
Tourist Info. Cen. —5G 23
(Paignton)
Tourist Info. Cen. —6D 8
(Shaldon)
Tourist Info. Cen. —5E 9
(Teignmouth)
Tourist Info. Cen. —6C 20
(Torquay)
Tourist Info. Cen. —4G 31
(Totnes)
Tower Rd. *Paign* —5E **23**
Town Clo. *Dart* —4B **30** (1A **30**)
Town Cotts. *Abbot* —1C **14**
Town Hall Pl. *Bov T* —2C **4**
*Town Quay. Tot —4G **31***
(off Plains)
Townsend Hill. *Ippn* —5A **14**
Townstal Cres. *Dart* —4A **30**
Townstal Hill. *Dart* —4B **30** (1A **30**)
Townstal Pathfields. *Dart* —4A **30**
Townstal Rd. *Dart* —4A **30**
Town Tree Hill. *Daw* —4D **2**
Tracey Va. *Bov T* —4B **4**
*Trafalgar Ter. Brix —1D **28***
(off Higher Furzeham Rd.)
Tramways. *Torq* —2C **20**
Treefields. *Brix* —3C **28**
Treesdale Clo. *Paign* —5C **22**
Trematon Av. *Torq* —4B **20**
Tremlett Gro. *Ippn* —5B **14**
Trentham Clo. *Paign* —3B **22**
Treston Clo. *Daw* —3E **3**
Treston Ho. *Daw* —3E **3**
Trevenn Dri. *Kgswl* —4H **15**
Triangle Pl. *Teign* —5E **9**
Triangle, The. *Teign* —5E **9**
Trinity Clo. *Teign* —3D **8**
Trinity Hill. *Torq* —6D **20**
Trough La. *Bov T* —2C **4**
Trumans Pl. *Daw* —4E **3**
Trumlands Rd. *Torq* —6F **17**
Truro Av. *Torq* —6F **17**
Tuckers Maltings. —2A 12
Tudor Clo. *Paign* —3D **24**
Tudor Rd. *New A* —2G **11**
Tuplins. *Kgstn* —3F **7**
Tweenaways. *Buckf* —5A **32**
Tweenways. *Kgstn* —4E **7**
Twickenham Rd. *New A* —3C **12**
Two Acre Clo. *Paign* —5B **22**

Underhill Rd. *Torq* —6H **19**
Underidge Clo. *Paign* —5B **22**
Underidge Dri. *Paign* —5B **22**
Underidge Rd. *Paign* —5B **22**
Under Way. *Kgswl* —1H **15**
Underwood Clo. *Daw* —6D **2**
Union La. *Brix* —2D **28**
Union Sq. Shop. Cen. *Torq* —4C **20**
Union St. *Dart* —1A **30**
Union St. *New A* —2G **11**
Union St. *Torq* —3A **20**
Uplands Rd. *Pres* —1D **22**
Up. Braddons Hill Rd. *Torq* —4D **20**
Up. Cockington La. *Torq* —3F **19**
Up. Headland Pk. Rd. *Pres* —2F **23**
Up. Hermosa Rd. *Teign* —4D **8**
Up. Longlands. *Daw* —3C **2**
Up. Manor Rd. *Paign* —3E **23**
Up. Morin Rd. *Paign* —4F **23**
Up. Penns Rd. *Pres* —2F **23**
Upton Hill. *Torq* —3B **20**
Upton Hill Rd. *Brix* —5D **28**
Upton Mnr. Pk. *Brix* —5D **28**
Upton Mnr. Rd. *Brix* —5C **28**
Upton Rd. *Torq* —3A **20**

Vale Clo. *Galm* —2E **27**
Valenia Ter. *Ashb* —4F **33**
Vale Rd. *Kgswl* —2H **15**
Vale Rd. *New A* —4A **12**
Valletort Clo. *Brix* —3B **28**
Valletort Pk. *Brix* —3B **28**
Valley Clo. *Teign* —2B **8**
Valley Path. *New A* —1D **10**
Valley Vw. Clo. *Torq* —2A **20**
Vanehill Rd. *Torq* —6D **20**
Vansittart Rd. *Torq* —3A **20**
Varian Ct. *Tot* —4H **31**
Vaughan Pde. *Torq* —6C **20**
Vaughan Rd. *Torq* —6C **20**
Vavasours Slip. *Dart* —3C **30**
Veille La. *Torq* —1F **19**
Velland Av. *Torq* —3E **17**
Venford Clo. *Paign* —5E **25**
Venture Ct. *New A* —2F **11**
Verbena Ter. *Shal* —6B **8**
Vernon Clo. *Torq* —6D **20**
Vicarage Clo. *Brix* —2D **28**
Vicarage Clo. *Sto G* —6A **24**
Vicarage Gdns. *Daw* —4C **2**
Vicarage Gro. *Sto G* —5A **24**
Vicarage Hill. *Brix* —2D **28**
Vicarage Hill. *Dart* —4B **30** (1A **30**)
Vicarage Hill. *Kgstn* —4F **7**
Vicarage Hill. *Torq* —5F **19**
Vicarage Hill. *Marl* —5A **18**
(Church Hill)
Vicarage Hill. *Marl* —6A **18**
(Five Lanes Rd.)
Vicarage Rd. *Abbot* —1C **14**
Vicarage Rd. *Brix* —4D **28**
Vicarage Rd. *Black & Sto G* —5A **24**
Vicarage Rd. *Torq* —5G **19**
Vicarage Rd. *Marl* —1B **22**
Vicary Clo. *New A* —2F **11**
Victoria Heights. *Dart* —4B **30**
Victoria Pde. *Torq* —6C **20**
Victoria Pk. Rd. *Torq* —2C **20**
Victoria Pl. *Dart* —4C **30** (1A **30**)
Victoria Pl. *New A* —2H **11**
Victoria Rd. *Brix* —1G **29**
Victoria Rd. *Dart* —4A **30** (1A **30**)
(in two parts)
Victoria Rd. *Torq* —3C **20**
Victoria Shop. Cen. *Paign* —5F **23**
Victoria St. *Paign* —5E **23**
Victoria St. *Tot* —4F **31**
Victoria Ter. *Kgstn* —4F **7**
*Victoria Ter. Shal —6C **8***
(off Bridge Rd.)
Victory Rd. *Dart* —4A **30**
Village Rd. *Marl* —6A **18**
Villiers Av. *New A* —3C **12**
Vine Rd. *Torq* —3A **20**
*Vinery, The. Torq —5C **20***
(off Montpellier Rd.)
Vittery Clo. *Brix* —2C **28**
Vomero. *Torq* —5D **20**

Waddeton Clo. *Paign* —4C **24**
Waddeton Cotts. *Wadd* —1B **26**
Waddeton Ind. Est. *Good* —4B **24**
Waddeton Rd. *Tot & Wadd* —1A **26**
Waddeton Rd. *Sto G* —5B **24**
Waddeton Rd. *Brix & Paign* —5C **24**
Wain La. *New A* —1F **11**
(in two parts)
*Waldon Ct. Torq —5C **20***
(off St Lukes Rd. S.)
*Waldon Point. Torq —5C **20***
(off St Luke's Rd. S.)
Walkham Ri. *Torq* —1E **19**
Wallace Av. *Daw* —3E **3**
Wallace Av. *Torq* —1F **19**
Wallaford Rd. *Buckf* —5A **32**
Wallfield Rd. *Bov T* —5A **4**
Wallis Gro. *Bish* —5H **9**
Wall Pk. Clo. *Brix* —2F **29**
Wall Pk. Holiday Cen. *Brix* —2G **29**
Wall Pk. Rd. *Brix* —2F **29**
Walls Hill Rd. *Torq* —2E **21**
Walnut Clo. *Tot* —3E **31**
*Walnut Ct. Brix —3E **29***
(off Higher Ranscombe Rd.)
Walnut La. *Torq* —5H **19**
Walnut Rd. *Torq* —5H **19**
Waltham Rd. *New A* —2F **11**
Warberry Rd. W. *Torq* —4C **20**
(in two parts)
Warberry Va. *Torq* —3C **20**
Warborough Rd. *Chur F* —1F **27**
Warbro Rd. *Torq* —2C **20**
Ware Barton Cvn. Site. *Kgstn* —5H **7**
Ware Clo. *Kgstn* —4G **7**
Warecroft Rd. *Kgstn* —4G **7**
Warecross Gdns. *Kgstn* —4G **7**
Warefield Rd. *Paign* —4F **23**
Warfleet Creek Rd. *Dart* —6D **30**
Warfleet Rd. *Dart* —5D **30**
Warland. *Tot* —4F **31**
Warren Hill. *Torq* —5C **20**
Warren Rd. *Daw & Daw W* —2G **3**
Warren Rd. *Torq* —5B **20**
Warren, The. *New A* —2E **11**
Warwick Clo. *Torq* —2F **21**
Washbourne Clo. *Brix* —2F **29**
Washington Clo. *Paign* —2E **23**
Watcombe Beach Rd. *Torq* —4H **17**
Watcombe Heights Rd. *Torq* —3G **17**
Waterdale Pk. *Kgswl* —3H **15**
Waterhead Clo. *Kgswr* —4D **30**
Water La. *Kgswl* —3H **15**
Water La. *New A* —1E **11**

Water La. *Torq* —1F **19**
Waterleat Av. *Paign* —6B **22**
Waterleat Clo. *Paign* —6C **22**
Waterleat Rd. *Paign* —6B **22**
Waterloo Rd. *Torq* —3C **20**
Waterloo St. *Teign* —5E **9**
Waterpool Rd. *Dart* —5A **30** (2A **30**)
Waterside. *Tot* —4G **31**
Waterside Holiday Camp. *Good* —4F **25**
Waterside Rd. *Paign* —4F **25**
Waterwell La. *New A* —5E **13**
Waverley Rd. *New A* —1G **11**
Wayside. *Brix* —3B **28**
Wayside Clo. *Brix* —3B **28**
Weaver Ct. *Torq* —1E **19**
Weavers Way. *Kgswl* —3G **15**
Webber Clo. *Ogwl* —5E **11**
Weech Clo. *Daw* —4C **2**
Weech Rd. *Daw* —4C **2**
Weekaborough Dri. *Marl* —1A **22**
Weeke Hill. *Dart* —6C **30**
Week La. *Daw & Daw W* —1F **3**
Weeksland Rd. *Torq* —3F **19**
Weirfields. *Tot* —3F **31**
Wellesley Rd. *Torq* —3C **20**
Wellington Pl. *Torq* —3C **20**
Wellington Rd. *Torq* —4C **20**
Wellington St. *Teign* —5E **9**
Well St. *Paign* —5D **22**
Wellswood Av. *Torq* —4E **21**
(in two parts)
Wellswood Gdns. *Torq* —4F **21**
Wellswood Pk. *Torq* —4E **21**
Wellswood Path. *Torq* —4E **21**
(in two parts)
Wembury Dri. *Torq* —5G **17**
Wentworth Rd. *Heath* —4E **5**
Wesley Clo. *Torq* —4F **17**
Wesley Ct. *Torq* —4F **17**
Wesley Vw. *Ippn* —5B **14**
Westabrook Av. *Ashb* —3E **33**
Westabrook Clo. *Ashb* —3E **33**
Westabrook Dri. *Ashb* —3E **33**
Westbourne Rd. *Torq* —2B **20**
W. Brook Av. *Teign* —4C **8**
W. Buckeridge. *Teign* —3D **8**
Westcliff. Daw —*4E* ***3***
(off Teignmouth Hill)
W. Cliff Clo. *Daw* —5D **2**
W. Cliff Pk. Dri. *Daw* —5D **2**
W. Cliff Rd. *Daw* —4C **2**
W. End Rd. *Buckf* —5A **32**
West End Ter. *Ashb* —5E **33**
Westerland La. *Marl* —1A **22**
Western By-Pass. *Tot* —5E **31**
Western Dri. *New A* —1E **11**
Western Rd. *New A* —3H **11**
Western Rd. *Torq* —6G **17**
Western Rd. *Ashb* —5E **33**
Western Ter. Tot —*4E* ***31***
(off Collins Rd.)
Western Vs. Tot —*4E* ***31***
(off Lwr. Collins Rd.)
Westfield Clo. *Brix* —4C **28**
Westhill Av. *Torq* —1C **20**
Westhill Av. Clo. *Torq* —2C **20**
Westhill Cres. *Paign* —4E **23**
Westhill Rd. *Paign* —4D **22**
Westhill Rd. *Torq* —1B **20**
Westhill Ter. *Kgswl* —3H **15**
Westlands La. *Torq* —2C **20**
West La. *Blag* —4A **18**
Westleat Av. *Paign* —5B **22**
West Mt. *New A* —4A **12**
Weston Clo. *Brix* —4D **28**
Westonfields. *Tot* —4H **31**
Weston La. *Tot* —4H **31**
Weston Rd. *Tot* —4G **31**
Westover Clo. *Brix* —3E **29**
W. Pafford Av. *Torq* —5F **17**
West St. *Bish* —5G **9**
West St. *Ashb* —4E **33**
West Town. *Bish* —5F **9**
W. Town Cotts. *Bish* —5F **9**
W. Town Mdw. *Bish* —5F **9**
West Vw. Clo. *Ogwl* —4E **11**
West Vw. Rd. *Marl* —6A **18**
Westward Arc. Tot —*4G* ***31***
(off Ticklemore St.)
Westward Clo. *Tot* —4F **31**
Westward Vw. *New A* —3D **12**
Westwood Rd. *Ogwl* —5F **11**
Wharf Rd. *New A* —1A **12**
Wheatlands Rd. *Paign* —1D **24**
Wheatridge La. *Torq* —1H **23**
Whidborne Av. *Torq* —6G **21**
Whidborne Clo. *Torq* —5G **21**
Whiddon Rd. *Abbot* —2A **14**
Whilborough Rd. *Kgswl* —6E **15**
Whistley Hill. *Ashb* —4F **33**
Whitear Clo. *Teign* —2B **8**
Whitears Way. *Kgstn* —4F **7**
Whitebeam Clo. *Paign* —4B **22**
White Clo. *Pres* —1E **23**
White Heather Ter. *Bov T* —2C **4**
Whitehill Clo. *New A* —6C **6**
Whitehill Cotts. *New A* —6A **6**
Whitehill Rd. *New A* —6A **6**
Whiteway Rd. *Kgstn* —4E **7**
Whitley Rd. *Paign* —1D **24**
Whitstone La. *Bov T* —2B **4**
Whitstone Rd. *Paign* —6E **23**
Widemoor La. *Galm* —3F **27**
Wilbarn Rd. *Paign* —4F **23**
Wilbury Way. *Daw* —3E **3**
Wildwoods Cres. *New A* —1C **12**
Willake Rd. *Kgswl* —2H **15**
Willhays Clo. *Kgstn* —2F **7**
Williams Clo. *Daw* —5C **2**
Williams Ct. *Buckf* —4B **32**
Willicombe Rd. *Paign* —6D **22**
Willis Ct. *Torq* —2B **20**
Willoughby Rd. *Torq* —3D **20**
Willow Av. *Torq* —4F **17**
Willow Clo. *New A* —5C **12**
Willowpark La. *Cof* —2B **16**
Willow St. *Teign* —5D **8**
Wills Av. *Paign* —2F **23**
Wills Rd. *Tot* —3G **31**
Wilton Clo. *Abbot* —1C **14**
Wilton Rd. *Pres* —1E **23**
Wilton Way. *Abbot* —1B **14**
Winchester Av. *Torq* —6E **17**
Windeatt Sq. Tot —*4G* ***31***
(off New Wlk.)
Windermere Rd. *Torq* —3D **20**
Winding Wlk. *Dart* —3C **30**
Windmill Av. *Paign* —2D **22**
Windmill Clo. *Brix* —3E **29**
Windmill Gdns. *Paign* —2D **22**
Windmill Hill. *Brix* —3D **28**
Windmill La. *Kgswl* —6E **15**
Windmill La. *Paign* —2C **22**
Windmill Rd. *Brix* —3E **29**
Windmill Rd. *Paign* —2D **22**
Windsor Av. *New A* —2C **12**
Windsor Clo. *New A* —3H **11**
Windsor Clo. *Torq* —3C **20**
Windsor Rd. *Dart* —4A **30**
Windsor Rd. *Torq* —3C **20**
Windthorn La. *Comp* —1A **18**
Windward La. *Daw* —1H **9**
Winner Hill Rd. *Paign* —5D **22**
Winner St. *Paign* —5D **22**
Winsford Rd. *Torq* —6F **19**
Winston Clo. *Kgstn* —4F **7**
Winston Ct. *Teign* —3E **9**
Winstone Av. *Torq* —6F **17**
Winsu Av. *Pres* —3D **22**
Winterbourne Rd. *Teign* —4D **8**
Winter Garden. *Torq* —5C **20**
Wishings Rd. *Brix* —4E **29**
Woburn Clo. *Paign* —4A **22**
Wolborough Chu. Path. *New A* —3F **11**
Wolborough Clo. *New A* —3H **11**
Wolborough Gdns. *Brix* —1F **29**
Wolborough St. *New A* —3F **11**
Wolston Clo. *Brix* —1C **28**
Wolverton Dri. *Kgstn* —4E **7**
Woodbrook Rd. *Tot* —4H **31**
Woodend Rd. *Torq* —5E **21**
Woodfield Ct. *Torq* —6E **21**
Woodland Av. *Kgswl* —2G **15**
Woodland Av. *Teign* —2F **9**
Woodland Clo. *Torq* —1H **19**
Woodland Gdns. Teign —*4E* ***9***
(off Lwr. Brimley)
Woodland Pk. *Paign* —4E **23**
Woodland Rd. *Torq* —1H **19**
Woodland Rd. *Ashb* —4F **33**
Woodlands Clo. *Teign* —4E **9**
Woodlands Gdns. *New A* —3C **12**
Woodlands Rd. *New A* —3C **12**
Wood La. *Abbot* —1B **14**
Wood La. *Kgswr* —4D **30**
Woodleigh Pk. *Shal* —6D **8**
Woodleigh Rd. *New A* —2E **11**
Woodmere Way. *Kgstn* —5F **7**
Woodpark La. *Comp* —1B **18**
Woodside Dri. *Torq* —5D **20**
Woods, The. *Torq* —6F **21**
Wood Vw. *New A* —2F **11**
Woodview Rd. *Paign* —4B **24**
Woodville Rd. *Torq* —3C **20**
Woodway Clo. *Teign* —2E **9**
Woodway Dri. *Teign* —3E **9**
Woodway Rd. *Teign* —2E **9**
Wordsworth Clo. *Torq* —3H **19**
Wren Ct. *Brix* —3D **28**
Wren Hill. *Brix* —3D **28**
Wright's La. *Torq* —2B **20**
Wrigwell La. *Ippn* —6C **14**
Wychwood Clo. *Daw* —3E **3**
Wyre Clo. *Paign* —3D **24**

Yalberton Ind. Est. *Paign* —1A **24**
Yalberton Rd. *Paign* —2A **24**
Yalberton Tor Ind. Est. *Paign* —2A **24**
Yannon Dri. *Teign* —3C **8**
Yannon La. *Kgswl* —2F **15**
(in two parts)
Yannons, The. *Teign* —3D **8**
Yannon Ter. *Teign* —3D **8**
Yards La. *Brix* —6C **28**
Yealm Gro. *Torq* —2F **19**
Yeolands, The. *Sto G* —5A **24**
Yew Clo. *Brix* —5A **28**
Yew Tree Dri. *Kgstn* —5F **7**
Yolhey La. *Abbot* —2D **14**
Yonder Mdw. *Sto G* —5A **24**
Yon St. *Kgswl* —3G **15**
York Cres. *Torq* —1D **20**
Yorke Rd. *Dart* —5A **30**
York Gdns. *Paign* —1E **25**
York Rd. *Paign* —1D **24**
York Rd. *Torq* —1D **20**
Young's Pk. Rd. *Paign* —1F **25**

Zion Pl. *Dart* —3C **30** (1A **30**)
Zion Rd. *Torq* —4A **20**